FALLEN IMAGES: EXPERIENCING DIVORCE IN THE MINISTRY

KEITH MADSEN

FALLEN IMAGES:
EXPERIENCING DIVORCE IN THE MINISTRY

KEITH MADSEN

Judson Press® *Valley Forge*

Library of Congress Cataloging in Publication Data
Madsen, Keith.
  Fallen images.

  Bibliography: p.
  1. Clergy—Divorce. 2. Clergy—Office.
3. Madsen, Keith. I. Title.
BV4395.5.M33 1985   253′.2   85-51
ISBN 0-8170-1076-9

Contents

71240

Preface

This is a book that is primarily about divorced ministers and their former spouses. But in a larger sense, it is a book about what it means to be a minister. It is a book about how a person's humanity is a part of ministry and how professional clergy and the church as a whole need to come to terms with the reality of that humanity and what it means for ministry. It is my hope, therefore, that this book will be read not only by divorced clergy and their churches but by all persons interested in a better understanding of the role of the professional minister.

This is not a book written from a strictly academic point of view. I myself am a divorced minister, my divorce having been finalized in February 1983. I have tried to share in a candid way what this experience has been like for me. I have also sought to share some of the meaning I have found in it.

While this book is born of my own experience, I have not relied totally on this in what I have written. To broaden my perspective I sent out a questionnaire (see Appendix A) to sixty divorced ministers across the country. Questionnaires were returned from forty-one of these ministers from eighteen different states and the District of Columbia. These states, with the number of responses from each, were: Washington (10), Oregon (9), California (4), Illinois (2), New York (2), Wisconsin (1), Massachusetts (1), Kentucky (1), Tennessee (1), Pennsylvania (1), Colorado (1), Utah (1), Kansas (1), New Jersey (1), New Hampshire (1), West Virginia (1), Connecticut (1), Indiana (1), and Washington, D.C. (1).

These responses have given me much information and insight. However, it must be admitted that this sample is not totally representative of all divorced ministers across the nation. There are three ways in which it is not a representative sample. (1) There is no representation from the South, where values are frequently more conservative. (2) Denominations represented are mainline denominations with a predominance of responses from American Baptists and United Methodists. The more conservative denominations, with the exception of the Southern Baptists, are not represented. (3) Respondents were contacted largely through denominational channels and hence do not include those who have left the ministry and with whom denominations no longer have formal contact.

While this sample is not representative of *all* divorced ministers, I believe it does give an informative picture of divorced ministers who remain in the ministry (or who are retaining contact with their denominations) and who minister in mainline denominations outside of the South.

In addition, I have sought to get information about former spouses of ministers. It was more difficult contacting such persons because their names and addresses are not as well known to denominational leaders. I did send out a questionnaire (see Appendix B) to thirteen former spouses of ministers. Of these, seven were returned. Information from these responses was combined with other research to form the basis for chapter 7.

Every effort has been made in this book to maintain nonsexist language and to recognize the growing number of women in the professional ministry. Seven female divorced ministers responded to my questionnaire. In addition, in some sections I have made general references to the minister as "him" or "her" alternately. I find this less awkward than the constant use of "him or her" or "him/her." However, where using just "him" or "her" might appear sexist, I have reverted to the use of "him or her."

In putting this book together, I have had much help. I especially want to thank Frank Brougher, pastor of the Spokane Valley Baptist Church in Spokane; Bob Burchel, my area minister; Mike Fitzgibbons, an Episcopal priest serving in Kennewick, Washington; the Seattle and Inland Empire Presbyteries; the Right Rev. Leigh A. Wallace, Jr., of the Episcopal Diocese of Spokane; and Rev. John Hierholzer, district superintendent for the United Methodist District of Spokane. Of course, I also want to thank the ministers and former spouses whose responses to my questionnaires have added so much to this book. Finally, I want to thank my wife, Cathy, and my stepdaughter, Jennifer, for being patient with me in the time I have needed to be away from them to accomplish this project.

An Increasing Trend

When I went to seminary in the early 1970s, I saw the main concern of the minister, in regard to divorce, as being how to help stem the tide of divorce in our country. Now, I see the minister's concern as being how to keep his or her own marriage strong in a world where more and more clergy are getting divorced. Clergy divorce is of special interest to me because in October 1982 I filed for divorce. The statistics of clergy divorce had become very personal. My former wife and I had struggled in our marriage for a long time, including a time of about a year and a half when we saw several marriage counselors in our efforts to pull things together. Finally, there came a time when I looked inside of myself and found that there just wasn't any spirit left in me to fight for a marriage I had come to see as bad for both of us. That was a hard decision. It was hard because we had been married for thirteen years, and there had been good times. It was hard because I believe God wants marriage to be permanent. It was hard because I knew that it would put stress on our lives and relationships for some time to come. But as hard as the decision was, I made it because I believed that God did not want that marriage to destroy us.

Filing for divorce was one of the most painful things I have ever done. As is true for many persons who divorce, it brought the pain of separation between me and my children and it brought tension to my relationship with my parents and other family members. It cut me off from relationships I had had with members of the family of my former wife, and that, too, was painful. But unlike people in most other professions, I also felt stress on my professional status. While many good people from the church I served were supportive, many were also confused and uneasy about how the divorce was going to affect my work as minister with youth. Would not this be a bad example? In truth, I struggled with that issue myself, both before and after my decision. This book comes as a result of my own struggles and my investigation into experiences of other divorced ministers.

Divorce is a highly charged, emotional topic. Since marriage and family is at the heart of our society and has a profound impact on our own emotional security, most of us see divorce as a frightening enemy. Divorce reminds us of the fragility of relationships that are very important to us. This is especially so when the person divorced is a highly visible figure like a minister.

Clergy divorce is part of an established trend toward divorce in our society as a whole. For a long time our society legislated to prevent divorce and also attached heavy moral stigmas to those who were involved. But as our society changed, the pressures of these changes led to an increase in divorce. People began to see marital breakdown as a tragedy that is made more traumatic by hard divorce laws which emotionalize issues and drag out the strain over a long time. So divorce laws were made more lenient, and the divorce rate continued to climb.

Moral stigmas have been eased along with those laws. When I was in high school it was pointed out to me at church that, while the divorce rate for marriages in general was one in every four marriages, the divorce rate for Christians who attended church regularly was negligible. It was impressed upon me that those who got divorced were those who lacked guiding moral principles and that if you had such principles, your marriage would most certainly thrive. Today, however, with the divorce rate around one in every three marriages, such views are changing. Gerald L. Dahl, in his 1981 book *Why Christian Marriages Are Breaking Up*, dealt with the reality that Christian marriages are no longer exempt from divorce. And in a three-year study of Minnesota Christians by the Institute for Ecumenical and Cultural Research (concluded in 1983), it was found that only 15 percent of the Christians surveyed considered divorce as always wrong or sinful.[1] Even as early as the late 1960s one sociological textbook could proclaim, "From being a rare example of moral disgrace, divorce has become a fairly common, more-or-less respectable way of dealing with an intolerable marriage."[2]

With this kind of increased moral acceptance of divorce, our churches are becoming full of people who either have been divorced themselves at some point or have experienced divorce in their immediate families. In the church where I minister, in the small, conservative town of Oakesdale, Washington, we recently had a Bible study during which we discussed divorce. In a poll of the people present, we found that all but two of the twelve people present had either been divorced themselves or had someone in their immediate family who was divorced. I don't believe this is unusual in churches today. The large number of divorced people has caused many churches to develop singles ministries, many of which seem to be dominated by people who have been divorced. Part of the thrust of these ministries is to help divorced persons to feel God's grace in their lives, to affirm themselves as persons of worth, and to see that they are just as much a part of the church's life and ministry as are married people.

The rise of clergy divorce, then, is part of an increasing trend toward divorce in our society as a whole. How widespread clergy divorce is now seems to be somewhat disputed. In her book *They Cry, Too!* Lucille Lavender made her oft-quoted statement that "among professionals, clergymen rank third in the number of divorces granted each year."[3] But others question that the rate is this high. Richard Goodling and Cheryl Smith, writing in the December 1983 issue of *The Journal of Pastoral Care*, indicated that the rate of divorce for pastors is significantly lower than for the general populace.[4] Dr. Paul Glick, senior demographer in the Population Division of the Bureau of Census, was quoted in David and Vera Mace's book *What's Happening to Clergy Marriages?* as saying that in 1960 the divorce rate for clergy was 0.2 percent and in 1970 it had doubled to 0.4 percent.[5] This is still significantly below the rate for the general population. Computing the number of clergy divorces is complicated by several factors. Denominational and Census Bureau surveys are limited by the ministers' desire for privacy about such information. Also, many clergy leave the ministry after a divorce and hence are no longer clergy. Still others probably leave the ministry because of marital problems that eventually result in divorce. As Mary LaGrand Bouma writes in *Divorce in the Parsonage*, "We will probably never know how many men have left the ministry for other professions because their marriages were in trouble."[6]

While the information on how the frequency of clergy divorce compares to the frequency of divorce in the general populace is disputed, there is no disagreement about the fact that clergy divorce is rapidly increasing in frequency. Divorce among the clergy used to be a rarity. It did happen. Even John Wesley, founding father of the Methodist Church, separated from his wife after twenty years of marriage. But the pressures against divorce among the clergy kept most ministers in marriages that others would have abandoned. Those who did divorce were hesitant to admit it. When Seward Hiltner did a survey of divorced ministers in 1958, he could find only seven who were willing to respond to his questionnaire.[7] But this hesitance among the clergy is now changing. Lyle Schaller says that the divorce rate for clergy has at least quadrupled since 1960.[8] And G. Lloyd Rediger indicates that 37 percent of the clergy with whom his counseling service works are seriously considering divorce.[9] Robert Stout definitely expressed the concensus when he wrote in the February 5, 1982, issue of *Christianity Today*, "There appears to be little doubt that there has been a recent trend toward divorce among clergy of all denominations."[10]

With the changes in the acceptability of divorce and with all of the pressures on marriage today, perhaps it should have been expected that divorce would hit the clergy as well. This should have been expected especially since ministers have pressures put on their marriages that are over and above the pressures put on other marriages. These include working many evenings and weekends when one's spouse is at home, living in a parsonage, where there is less privacy than in a privately owned home, living with low pay, and being expected to live up to certain roles which may or may not fit the individual.

In spite of these reasons why clergy divorce should have been expected, the rise in clergy divorce is a trend that is disturbing the church deeply. Whereas today the laity have come to accept divorce as a fact of life for people in general, they do not have the same acceptance for divorce among the clergy. Somehow more is expected of ministers, and if they don't live up to those expectations, they suffer a considerable loss of prestige. David and Vera Mace write, "A pastor involved in separation or divorce, apart from a very few atypical exceptions, plummets to the lowest level of public esteem."[11] While reactions from the divorced clergy with whom I have communicated indicate that this loss of respect may not occur as often as the Maces imply, it does happen in many cases. And when it does, the loss of esteem can be devastating to the minister. Some ministers lose their church positions. In many denominations if a minister is divorced, this most certainly hurts one's ability to get appointments or to receive a call from another church. When I was searching for a church after my divorce, regional executives in my denomination warned me that many churches of their area do not accept divorced ministers, especially if they are not remarried. Some ministers in other denominations have found that those who are the least accepting of their divorces are not lay people. Instead they are their peers and the people in the church hierarchy who have the greatest influence on their getting other positions.[12] One minister, who was working as an associate pastor at the time of his divorce, found that his senior pastor—who has a reputation in ministry to the divorced and single—was not very accepting of divorce when it involved his own staff. When the associate first told his senior pastor about the possibility of his marriage ending in divorce, the senior pastor told him that he did not know whether he could accept a minister who had been divorced, in the position of associate. It is likely that other senior pastors who have had fewer dealings with ministry to the divorced would have been even less tolerant. One minister from Wisconsin found his supervisor to be very critical when he went through just a time of marital separation.

Why is it that clergy divorce is met with such intolerance in a society that seemingly has learned to accept divorce as an unfortunate side effect of our humanity? It seems to me that the stress caused by clergy divorce comes from three sources. First of all, the pastor and other ministers on staff are like family for many members of the church. Just as a person's family suffers stress when a member is divorced, the same occurs in the church when one of their ministers is divorced. Ministers who divorce need to expect this reaction. The grief of a church over such an occurrence often has to be attended to for some time after the event. We will deal more fully with this later. But such is not the full reason why clergy divorce seems to be thought of differently than divorce in general, for this factor says nothing of why churches are often hesitant to accept a minister who has already been divorced.

A second reason why clergy divorce causes more stress than other divorce is that clergy are viewed as the last bastion of defense against the onslaught of divorce. In spite of the fact that we are more accepting of divorce today, we still realize its potential to hurt and destroy. We feel that if even the clergy are being divorced (although in lower percentages), then nobody is safe. When my wife and I were divorced, it was at a time when a popular song asked whether anyone ever stayed in love anymore. A good friend told me that this song spoke to feelings she had about my divorce. If my former wife and I could be divorced, then it could happen to anyone and the whole idea of a lifelong, fulfilling marriage was in jeopardy. While our friend reacted in this way in part because she had experienced us as friends, it seems to me that clergy, especially, are expected to serve in a somewhat mythological way as protectors against the divorce threat.

While it is difficult to see how a minister's happy marriage would in any significant way protect other marriages from divorce, it is certainly understandable that people want such a sense of protection. The pain of divorce is all too obvious. And it is scary at times to see all of the people who are divorced. Even those of us who have been divorced and have felt that the end result was for the best, know that the hurt divorce brings makes it difficult to defend. At best, we can say that the final resolution of the problem is worth the pain.

Another reason for special concern over clergy divorce is the conviction, which still remains with us, that divorce is not what God wants for us. Marriage is to last forever. Does not Malachi 2:16 tell us that God hates divorce? Even though lay people and non-Christians may not live up to this ideal, ministers *must* do so in order to proclaim God's will for marriage. Ministers are to proclaim the sanctity of marriage with their lives as well as with their words.

It is my belief that clergy *do* need to proclaim God's will with their lives as well as with their words. And I would also agree wholeheartedly that God's will for marriage is that it be a lifelong commitment. But that is not the sum total of all that God wills for marriage. God also wants it to be a life-enhancing relationship. One does not properly model God's will for marriage simply by sticking it out to the end in a destructive relationship.

Nevertheless, the need for ministers to proclaim what God wants in marriage in a total way is a legitimate concern that should be shared by minister and congregation alike, including those ministers who have gone through divorce. How can a minister be an example in the midst of his or her own divorce? As we look at this issue together in the

Divorce
how you make me
bleed
as you carry
me along
in your swirl
of
Death
and
Resurrection.
You slash apart troubled souls
and don't even sear
the stumps.
If you could but
erase
my mistake
more painlessly
I could speak
with more affinity
to those
who call you
Enemy.

chapters that follow, I will show how there are two approaches to the question of the minister-as-example. One is the minister-as-image. This approach requires the minister to seek to project herself or himself as the embodiment of all that she or he proclaims. This understanding can be a tremendous burden on all ministers, divorced or not, and frequently results in defeat. The other approach is the minister-as-model. This approach means that the minister needs to model the truths of the gospel, including the truths of human fallibility and need for grace. He or she needs to show that in the midst of very real sinfulness, we can still have spiritual strength and we can still be God's children.

As we come to a greater understanding of the minister-as-example, I believe we will find that divorced ministers *can* still exemplify what God calls us to do and be.

The Minister as Image

Practice what you preach!'' No other saying related to the ministry is used more widely than this. Most of us have heard this since we were children. It conveys the conviction that persons who preach the gospel (or any other message, for that matter) should proclaim the same concepts in their living as they proclaim in their words. The minister who preaches to others should be a living example of what he or she is saying. Does not this requirement leave the divorced minister condemned as a failure in the crucial role of marriage? Certainly ministers proclaim marriage as a sacred and eternal bond. When their own marriages fail, have they not failed as examples?

The divorced minister cannot reject the fact that the requirement of being an example is valid. It is well-grounded in the Bible. In 1 Peter 5:2-3, we are told that the clergy should "shepherd the flock of God among you, not . . . lording it over those allotted to your charge, but proving to be examples to the flock." And Timothy was advised, ". . . In speech, conduct, love, faith and purity, show yourself an example of those who believe" (1 Timothy 4:12). The appeal could arguably be extended to apply to all pastors. Certainly the tone of 1 Timothy, chapter 4, would seem to indicate that the author saw the importance of the minister-as-example.

The need for the minister to be an example also has great importance theologically. A central tenet of our faith is that God could not really be encountered in abstraction but had to take on flesh and blood, in the person of Jesus Christ, in order for people to understand God's love.

Similarly, people have a hard time understanding how to apply God's Word to their lives unless they see the principles that are taught to them incarnate in someone else. If that person is not their minister, who is it to be? For these reasons it is understandable that the ordained minister is expected to be an example, and that many perceive this to mean that his or her standards should be higher than the accepted standards of society in general.

While the divorced minister cannot avoid this role of example, it does not necessarily follow that she or he stands condemned by it. The question becomes what this status implies about a minister's behavior. Certainly one view is that a minister cannot show any major moral flaw or failure. The minister has to project the Image of a person who has been strong enough to resist the evils with which others struggle. Such a view holds that only the one whom others see as totally victorious will be respected as an example. I call this view "the minister-as-Image."

The view of the "minister-as-Image" has a strong following in traditional Christian views of what a minister should be. Raymond Calkins, in his 1944 book, *The Romance of the Ministry*, champions this approach. He writes, "Perfection . . . is precisely what is demanded of the minister."[1] He goes on to explain,

> It is demanded of the minister that his life shall be above reproach. The moral standards of the ministry are high and they are inexorable. Maltie D. Babcock once said that a minister's life must not only be clean, it must be antiseptic. The slightest deviation from the implacable rules which govern a minister's conduct brings down upon him final condemnation. It should be a matter of pride in the profession of the ministry that this is so."[2]

Calkins summed up his views by saying, "People as a whole think of their ministers, and have a right to think of them, as being incapable of immoral conduct in any form."[3]

Today, most people probably do not go quite as far as Calkins suggests, at least at the conscious, rational level. On the rational level, most would acknowledge that even ministers make mistakes. Certainly anyone familiar with the Bible knows that "all have sinned and fall short of the glory of God." But at a *feeling* level there is still often the expectation that the minister is above the moral struggles of the rest of humanity. I even remember that when I first learned about sex in junior high, one of my first reactions was "Surely our *minister* wouldn't do such a thing—even with his wife!"

Many of those people who admit moral imperfection in the minister expect it not to go beyond acts that are just barely bad enough to be considered sinful at all. Sure, the minister probably *occasionally* says a "bad word" when he hits his thumb with a hammer. Or maybe she sometimes forgets to pray or read her Bible when she is supposed to. Or perhaps the minister even has a moment or two of doubt when faith is questioned. But the "big" sins have all been conquered. And if they have not, then at least it should appear that way.

With all the requirements of the "minister-as-Image," there is no doubt that the divorced minister falls short of what is expected. Divorce means moral failure. It means failure to sustain over a lifetime the kind of love God calls for in a marriage. It is not a little moral failure. It's a big one. And worst of all, it is "disgustingly obvious."

For the divorced minister, perhaps the most painful part of all this is that at the same time he is falling short of the "Image" much of his congregation has required, the "Image" he has built of himself is also being shattered. David and Vera Mace, in discussing the pressures put upon clergy and their spouses by high expectations, write,

> The main reason why many clergy couples so strongly resent having high congregational expectations imposed upon them is because this touches them at a very sensitive spot—the distressing and exasperating fact that they secretly cherish the same high expectations for themselves, but have not yet been able to realize them.[4]

Divorce forces a minister to acknowledge her own sinfulness to herself as well as to others.

Divorce also necessitates behavior that is counter to the self-image most ministers have. Ministers typically see themselves as sensitive, caring individuals who want to be perceived as giving to and serving others. John Landgraf describes the typical minister as "keenly sensitive to interpersonal interactions, particularly as to how he is received in an acceptance-rejection way."[5] When such a person goes through divorce, which typically includes much hostility and anger, this self-image takes a beating. A minister from Utah wrote, "I felt like a failure for a period of time, and thought that since I was basically a nice guy who did things 'right,' this should not have happened to me." It was not uncommon for these self-image issues to cause the ministers with whom

I communicated to question their calling. A minister from Wisconsin wrote, "I didn't know how I could 'proclaim the Good News' without experiencing it." Another minister, from western Washington, wrote, ". . . I felt I would never again be a minister." Of course, ministers also struggle with self-image issues which don't necessarily relate to their being ministers and with which other divorced persons struggle. The minister from western Washington also wrote, "I felt unwanted, unattractive, a failure at being a husband—a man. . . ." An Episcopal minister shared, "At first I was scared and felt like a failure—covered over with the facade of 'Everything's just fine!' " And a minister in a denominational position in Washington wrote that he still struggles with the image of being "a divorced person" even thirteen years after his divorce. These self-image problems make it difficult for ministers to see themselves in the exalted way they are used to being seen by the public. They have to let go of the false Image of themselves that has been an ego boost.

In my own case, my filing for divorce had a profound effect on my self-image. I had always seen myself as a person who helps people rather than hurts them. Like the minister from Utah, I was a "nice guy." But when I filed for divorce, I was suddenly surrounded by people who were hurt as a result. My former wife felt hurt and rejected. My children were hurt because it meant insecurity and possible separation from me. My parents were hurt because my ex-wife was family and because they felt what I was doing was wrong. Certainly, I came to a realization that sometimes a person has to do what is best for one's self to protect one's emotional health, even when others are hurt in the midst of that. One cannot go through life basing decisions solely on avoiding hurting others. But the Image I had of myself, of one who could never do something that resulted in someone else being hurt, had to fall. So did another part of the "Image." My parents, especially my mother, had always pointed at me as an example of what my brothers and sisters should be. While I always have been uncomfortable with being used in this way, there was also a part of me that found it a boost for my ego. With the divorce, that part of the Image also fell.

With counseling I was able to take a new look at the false view of myself that I had accepted. Like others, I viewed myself as a "good guy" who was always in control of his negative emotions. I was always patient and never got angry. Or at least that is what I wanted to portray

Who are you
            now,
      you stranger
               inside of me?
No longer
      the one who
            does the Good—
            the official family
                  Example
                  for all who needed such.
No longer
      giver
      to all,
            hoping
                  to receive.
Who are you
      now
      that
            you are no longer
            defined
      by
            Others?

to myself and others. But my anger was there. It was real and it was deep and it was *very* human. I had to stop seeing myself as one who always considered only others and never myself. I had to show myself that I had to consider and share my own needs sometimes in order to be human, instead of being the "super-servant" I had expected myself to be. And once I had humanized *my* view of myself, I could more easily understand that my family's view of me could be similarly transformed.

The reality, then, is that while many ministers are uncomfortable with the "Image" demanded by others, that "Image" also fills ego needs and helps them deceive themselves at times into thinking that maybe they really are as good as others say they are supposed to be.

While the "Image" serves an ego function for the minister, it also serves some functions for others as well. Of course, the function it is supposed to serve is that of example. When the people see their minister living a life of moral strength and purity, they are supposed to be inspired to do the same. This is certainly an important function, as I noted earlier. But when the minister is seen as essentially without flaw in that moral strength and purity, the function of example is undermined because the lay person is acutely aware of his or her own failures and knows that she or he can never measure up to such an example. When what someone needs is an example, then, the minister-as-Image can only produce frustration and even despair in the lay person.

Another function the "Image" performs is to provide the layperson with a source of vicarious righteousness. When a layperson is frustrated by his own moral failures and weaknesses, he can find some solace in his identification with "his" minister who will be righteous *for* him. Perhaps too, there is the feeling present that the "obvious strength" of the minister will be able, at least partially, to protect such a person from his own weakness, like a parent protecting a child. Such dynamics were seen in extreme in the case of cult leader Jim Jones and his followers a few years back. But they can also be seen in the large followings of many nationally known preachers who project themselves in an authoritarian, self-righteous way. The followers of such persons are threatened by any indication of cracks in the "Image."

Fortunately, most lay people are not so insecure. But sometimes it takes only a few people in a church demanding that the minister live the "Image" to make things uneasy for the minister who wants to get out of that role.

It seems to me that persons who demand a minister who conforms to the Image are like those persons Paul encountered at Lystra. The situation is described in Acts 14:11-18:

> And when the multitudes saw what Paul had done, they raised their voice, saying in the Lycaonian language, "The gods have become like men and have come down to us." And they began calling Barnabas, Zeus, and Paul, Hermes, because he was the chief speaker. . . . But when the apostles, Barnabas and Paul, heard of it, they tore their robes and rushed out into the crowd, crying out and saying, "Men, why are you doing these things? We are also men of the same nature as you. . . ." And even saying these things, they with difficulty restrained the crowds from offering sacrifices to them.

If people want the Image, they will get the Image! It's hard for some to accept ministers who proclaim themselves as "men [or women] of the same nature" as they are. In Oakesdale, the small community in which I minister, some of the men of the community get together every day for coffee. To determine who pays for the coffee they play a guessing game called "Hi-Lo." While the loser has to pay for coffee for all, he also gets to run the next game. One day another man offered to take the last guess and so lose in my place. He said, "I'll take it. After all, I can take revenge on them for 'sticking' me, but you can't."

I have not cited this example to say anything bad about the man who made that comment, since he is a very likeable person. But, rather, I wanted to illustrate that lay people often see ministers as "playing with a different set of rules." Is the minister to avoid revenge (even in a game!) as an example to others that they can be expected to follow? Not necessarily! The layperson has no intention of laying such a burden on himself. Rather, the minister is to behave in such a manner to maintain the flawless Image.

For clergy to minister to others as "people of the same nature," the Image has to fall. It must fall for several reasons. First of all, the Image is a poor way of fulfilling the function of example to the people, as has already been pointed out. In fact, it can be seen as setting a poor example. The minister is called to live out the gospel, not to embody the slavery of legalism! And the legalism of the Image does enslave the minister in several ways. Because ministers are to care for all people equally, there are those who invoke the Image to say that ministers are to have no special friends in the church. Having special friends might be perceived as favoritism! If even a minority of the membership frowns on dancing, the minister can't dance. If even a minority of the membership frowns on drinking, the minister can't drink. How can a minister proclaim the freedom of the gospel when she is enslaved to the legalism of the Image?

Another point about the Image as legalism is that, like all legalisms, it's not applied to all actions equally. A divorce shatters the Image. But what about becoming dictatorial in one's pastoral leadership style? It is this that Peter refers to specifically in the passage cited at the beginning of this chapter. He says, "Shepherd the flock of God among you, not . . . as lording it over those allotted to your charge, but proving to be examples to the flock." Even so, a dictatorial pastor is more likely to be accepted than a divorced one!

The minister who buys into the Image is also setting a poor example by being false. As David and Vera Mace write,

> When people in public office find that they cannot measure up to idealized expectations of those whom they represent, they are often forced to conceal their shortcomings and build around themselves a system of defenses and pretenses. The result is that soon the outward appearance comes to be accepted as reality, and the only way to maintain status is by putting on an act.[6]

A minister who, in order to live up to the morally pure Image, will not show himself as he is, with all his imperfection, is sending a message to others to do the same. How, then, can there be genuine relating in the church when everyone is false?

Perhaps the most crucial reason why the Image must fall is that its function of providing vicarious righteousness has already been done. That's what Christ was all about! He was the sinless one who alone could be presented as a sacrifice before God "once for all." It is Christ with whom we must identify in order for his righteousness to be claimed as ours. The minister who allows herself to be put in that role is diverting attention from Christ as the central figure of our faith!

Robert Stout writes, "We need to rid ourselves of the 'halo effect.' Those who are ordained are neither perfect nor infallible."[7] As such, a concept of the minister-as-example that does not allow for moral imperfection cannot be seen as helpful. We need to say with Paul, "We are also persons of the same nature as you. . . ." And then, from our positions as fellow strugglers, we need to redefine what it means to be an example.

From Image to Model

If the minister is called to be an example and if, as I have maintained, the view of the minister as the flawless "Image" is an inadequate concept of example, then a different concept must be outlined. For a concept of minister-as-example to be adequate, it must do three things: (1) it must encourage people to reach for a higher plane in their spiritual growth; (2) it must be something the minister can accomplish without the necessity of deception; and (3) it must show other people what they really can attain. While the view of "minister-as-Image" accomplishes the first of these (assuming people don't get discouraged reaching for the impossible), it fails on the latter two counts.

A more adequate view of the clergy's status of being an example is what I call the "minister-as-model." The words "model" and "image" connote different ideas. "Image" has the connotation of something artificially shaped into the appearance of perfection. Such falseness is often worshiped by those who are disillusioned with that which is living and real. In Bible times people worshiped false images that had flawless appearances but that did not have the reality of the living God. In the same way, people often gravitate toward false human images because they are disillusioned with living, real human beings. This is the appeal of Hollywood celebrities, sports stars, some political figures, and too many ministers. But falseness is falseness, whether we are dealing in the human or the divine.

The term "model" has the connotation of a living, breathing human being who shows the best of what is possible. Those in the church need to move toward affirming the concept of "minister-as-model." Such a concept needs to be based on two differences with the view of "minister-as-Image." First of all, it should be based on the idea that a minister can be an example, not because he or she has no *weaknesses*, but because he or she has recognizable *strengths*, which the Christian community needs. Divorced ministers most certainly have manifested weaknesses that have resulted in divorce. But their adequacy as examples is based on the adequacy of their strengths.

The divorced ministers who responded to my questionnaire most certainly have strengths, as is evidenced by their present positions and activities. Respondents include several persons now holding denominational staff positions, several who are now working as counselors in church-related institutions, as well as persons who are pastors or associate pastors of churches of all sizes. Two of them have had books published, one on pastoral care to singles and one on marriage.

The central tragedy of how divorced ministers have frequently been treated in the past is that much talent has been wasted because the church has rejected a person solely because of a divorce. A minister can be a tremendous preacher, she can demonstrate the greatest skill and tenderness in dealing with the mourning of people at the time of a death, he can be a skilled community leader in bringing about social justice—but if he or she gets a divorce, his or her ministry is viewed as over! Does Christ really have so many skilled people doing his work that he can afford this waste?

This is not to say that a person's weaknesses are unimportant. Obviously, even if a person can preach like Billy Graham and has the compassion of Mother Teresa, it is still a grave concern if he is in the habit of running through town naked in broad daylight! And so a second difference our view of minister-as-model must have from the view of "minister-as-Image" is that a minister, in order to be a good example, must deal with her weaknesses with forthrightness and courage. She does not cover them up and pretend they do not exist. Ministers lose effectiveness when they have to expend energy hiding an "Achilles heel"! Nor can a person act as if those weaknesses are totally unimportant.

A good example of facing weaknesses courageously was provided for me by Darrell Porter when he was catcher for the Kansas City Royals a few years ago. Since sports figures are examples for young

Lord,
    I don't want
  to be
        a Holy Man—
Pray-er
        of
        official-sounding
                prayers
Dispenser
        of
        Holy Words
                for all occasions
Blesser
        of all
        that cannot find
                a blessing
        within itself.
Lord,
    I don't want
  to be
        a Holy Man—
Shining
        in some High Holy Place
    for all to see
                on Holy Days
        for all to see
                but
                not
                    to
                touch.

Lord,
    I don't want
  to be
        a Holy Man—

Stripped
    of my
    right
        to imperfection
Stripped
    of the
    human needs
        that well up
        from
    deep
        within my soul.

Lord,
    I don't want
    to be
        a Holy Man—
But Lord
        I do so want to be
        Your Man—
To touch
        the ones
        You call me
            to touch
To hear
        Your Word
        whispered
            in the lives
        around me
To feel
        the need
        of all
            Your Holy Children
        when they cry.

Lord,
I don't want
to be
a Holy Man—
I
just
want
to be
Wholly human
Wholly alive
and
Most of all
Wholly Yours.

boys and girls, it causes somewhat of a problem when their personal weaknesses are made manifest. Darrell Porter was struggling increasingly with an alcohol problem. At first he tried to hide it, as do most people with such problems. But then in the middle of the baseball season, he decided to meet the problem head-on by enrolling in an alcohol treatment program. Of course, that meant that he was out of the Royals' lineup for a while. But while alcoholism is certainly not consistent with a positive image of a professional ball player, the citizenry of Kansas City gained the utmost respect for Porter because of his courage in facing his weakness. When he returned to the lineup he was met with a standing ovation! Such was his popularity that when the Royals traded him to the St. Louis Cardinals, the trade was very unpopular. Kansas City fans were among those who cheered the loudest when Porter starred in the World Series a couple of years later. Darrell Porter had fallen from the image the professional ball player was supposed to have. But he had become a well-respected model!

A minister's role as model, then, is similar to the role Ronald Sider and Richard Taylor say the church should play in working for world peace. They write in their book *Nuclear Holocaust and Christian Hope*:

> Christians have a hopeful word of peace for our dangerous world. But if we have not allowed the Holy Spirit to heal the dividing walls in our churches, we will not be heard.
> This does not mean that local congregations must be perfect examples of peace and harmony before they can undertake significant action for peace . . . . But it *does* mean that we must open ourselves again and again to the peace and reconciliation which Jesus gives. . . . It means that we cry and confess when we fail. It means that we resolve anew to offer Christ's costly, self-sacrificial love to the most difficult members of our fellowship.[1]

The key ideas in this approach are: (1) commitment to live out the teaching, (2) acknowledgment and mourning of the failure, and (3) recommitment to the task. Ministers who seek to be models should then commit themselves to living out what they preach. They should be free to acknowledge and confess their failures, and they should be willing to recommit themselves continually to their tasks as models by addressing their weaknesses with openness and courage.

After the qualifications for being a model have been outlined, it should be clear that divorced ministers are as qualified to be models as are ministers whose failures or weaknesses are shown in other ways. Divorce, while tragic, *can* also be evidence that the minister has the courage to face a frightening reality and act accordingly. Many people stay with marriages, not because they have any real expectation that problems will be made manageable and the marriage will be good, but because they are afraid of taking the risk of change.

Certainly, some people's choice of divorce is made irresponsibly and can be categorized as fleeing difficult problems that could have been handled if faced. But the evidence is that this, as a rule, is not the case with ministers. De Forest Wiksten, an area director for the United Methodist Church who dealt with thirty clergy marriages that ended in divorce, was quoted in the Maces' *What's Happening to Clergy Marriages?* as saying of clergy divorce, "I never say one in which the pastor was irresponsible in approaching it. There was enormous pain, agony, and endless struggle to work through to a solution."[2] This is probably somewhat of an overstatement, especially since there are clergy divorces in which the partners make no effort at finding counseling. But it is a significant affirmation nonetheless. Seward Hiltner made a similar point in his 1958 article, saying, "In every instance the divorce was delayed at least in part because the man was a minister. . . . All our ministers counsel caution on divorce, which is to be seen as a last resort."[3]

Reports from the divorced ministers with whom I corresponded are consistent with Hiltner's statement. One minister, now in a denominational position in Washington State, said that in the first years of his married life he and his former spouse had two years of marital counseling. In retrospect, he believes he should have seen at the time that the extended counseling indicated divorce as the best option, but he held back because he believed that divorce was a sin. He explained to me, "We were in trouble from the very beginning. I felt great pressure in the early years to maintain the troubled relationship because 'What else could I do?' Later, the load was too heavy and I had to risk the divorce." His marriage lasted twelve years. In another case, a Presbyterian minister from the state of Washington wrote me of how he and his former spouse had gone through thirty-seven years of a marriage which was troubled throughout. The marital disharmony was apparently a factor in several lost ministerial opportunities. The couple had even separated for several months as early as 1956. By 1966 he was having difficulty getting a full-time pastorate because of his marital problems, and so he became bivocational with a part-time pastorate. In 1977 he came to the conclusion that divorce would be necessary, but he backed off from taking action because he wanted to wait until their youngest child was married and settled down. Finally, he filed for divorce in 1983 after thirty-seven years of marriage. While such reports need to be understood as somewhat partial, they indicate genuine effort on the part of these divorced ministers and their former spouses.

In my own case, my former wife and I attempted to pull our marriage together by instituting "family nights" and "logging in" sessions to share feelings and pray, by spending weekends alone together, by participating in a weekend marriage-growth experience for clergy, and by going to counseling for about a year and a half. All of these efforts helped, even though they did not save the marriage in the end. Our marriage lasted thirteen years. In all, the average length of the marriages of the divorced clergy with whom I corresponded was 16.5 years. This also indicates that ministers (at least those who stay in the ministry) do not give up on their marriages easily or quickly.

If divorce is sometimes a necessary option for people in general, and from the study of Minnesota Christians cited in chapter 1 it would seem that most Christians believe it is, then "modeling" may mean showing how to come to the decision to divorce and how to proceed through the divorce in a responsible way. Ministers who divorce can even be models in the process of divorce if they make genuine efforts to heal the marriage first. Such modeling should include sharing the marital struggle with at least some church family members so they can be available for support. Modeling should also include confronting the issues in the marriage through participating in marriage counseling, using community or denominational resources, and giving plenty of time and prayer to finding healing in the marriage. If ministers whose marriages are in trouble would take such steps, they would set an example for others that would help reduce the divorce rate in our country, even if it turned out their own marriages could not be saved.

There are other ways in which divorced ministers may have unique opportunities to serve as models. One such opportunity is in the area of stepparenting. Christians who are divorced and remarried are in need of leaders who can teach and model how to confront the problems that arise in stepparenting. David and Bonnie Juroe note in their book *Successful Stepparenting* that "trying to blend broken families may possibly be the most serious and complex social and mental health crisis affecting children in the eighties."[4] Not all divorced ministers will have such skills. But those who remarry and do have such abilities will provide vital role models for other stepparents.

A need also exists for Christians to model what it means to live responsibly as adult singles in today's world. Too often singles are seen by married people as irresponsible. Single pastors can show people that this is not necessarily so, and they can provide Christian singles with role models as well.

I am not saying here that ministers need to divorce to gain new opportunities to be models. Rather, I am saying that when a minister's marriage tragically ends, the Christian community need not treat the divorce as destroying his or her function as an "example to the flock." But instead, both minister and congregation need to affirm the minister's humanity, look at the strengths which remain, and be open to the many ways the minister can fulfill an exemplary role.

Modeling and Clergy Marriage

Marriage is an important arena of life, and as such, it is an area in which modeling is vitally needed. But given the understanding of modeling we developed in the last chapter, there is no reason to say that divorced ministers have completely failed at this function, any more than one could say automatically that ministers who remain married are succeeding. Divorced ministers *have* failed to maintain their marriages over a lifetime. But success or failure as a model should be related to how well a person is doing things that strengthen marriage and avoiding doing things that weaken it. When one looks at modeling this way, one can see that there are a disturbingly large number of ministers, some who remain married and some who have divorced, who are not doing a very good job of modeling in the area of marriage.

When a divorce occurs, it becomes obvious that mistakes have been made in the marital relationship. But the mere fact that a divorce has not occurred does not in any way mean that such mistakes are being avoided. As marriage counselors David and Vera Mace have written, "The outside appearance of stability in marriages provides us with no clear indication of how healthy or unhealthy the relationships are on the inside."[1] In fact, the marriages of many clergy couples show serious shortcomings that hurt their attempts to be models. In regard to clergy marriages the Maces have noted, "For some years we ourselves deeply engaged in the marriage enrichment movement, have been discovering that many of the clergy couples who came to our weekend retreats had quite superficial relationships."[2] And the Maces are not the only ones who see it that way. John Landgraf, who works in counseling at the Center of the Ministry in Oakland, California, writes, "I have marvelled at how often ministerial marriages can accurately be characterized as 'two people living alone together.' "[3] Certainly, there are many sound clergy marriages in which love is alive and well. But the number of clergy marriages for which this is not the case is cause for concern, regardless of whether those marriages end in divorce.

There are many reasons why clergy marriages are having difficulty. Some of those reasons are the same reasons why other marriages are having trouble. Donna Sinclair, herself a minister's wife, has discovered that "clergy marriages are subject to the same dynamics as everybody else's. One partner may outgrow the other. They may have been immature at the beginning, and eventually grew up different."[4] Others point out the role of life passages in clergy marital stress.[5]

Problems in clergy marriage can also relate to the stress of being in the ministry. While Donna Sinclair reports that few of the former wives of clergy she interviewed blamed the breakdown of their marriage on church-related issues, she nevertheless points out that such issues are often complicating factors.[6] Several of the ministers who answered my questionnaire made specific references to church stresses playing a part in their marital struggles, which led to divorce.

One Methodist minister now serving a special appointment referred to the stress of living in a parsonage, noting that it was hard on his former wife living "in the literal shadow of the church." This was especially true since she wanted some improvements made, which were denied, and she wanted to convert to a housing allowance, which was also denied. Living in a parsonage can bring stress to a marriage because many church people see the house as theirs and hence feel they should be able to use it in any way they see fit. Some church people come into the parsonage unannounced. Others feel the pastor is obligated to use the parsonage for all kinds of functions, from holding Sunday school classes to babysitting during church meetings. The pastor's family are frequently denied requests for remodeling because some people feel the next pastor may not like the changes. The result is that the parsonage does not really feel like home to the pastor's family, and the family members do not feel they have the privacy any family needs. Mary LaGrand Bouma reports that because of such problems,

A psychologist who has been a pastor and who has counseled a great many pastors and their wives over the years is quite outspoken about telling congregations to keep hands off the parsonage. He believes that this abuse of the pastor's house has been a factor in the precarious mental health of many wives.[7]

Others referred to the stress caused by spouses who did not want their mates in the ministry. A Methodist minister from a western state wrote, "My wife had become antagonistic toward the church and resentful of my desire to return to parish pastoral ministry at reduced pay after several successful years in social service work." A Baptist minister wrote that his former wife "never enjoyed being a minister's wife once she got into it and got progressively more and more negative about it." He went on to say that the amount of time that church problems and emergencies took up was a source of regular tension in the relationship. A minister serving an Episcopal congregation in the northwest wrote, "My involvement in the church was something my ex-husband felt some jealousy toward (perhaps irrationally because I was rather careful to leave plenty of family time.)" The demands of a church on family time are certainly great, and since people differ in how much family time they feel is enough, it is understandable that this would be a prime area for conflict in clergy marriage.

Several fine studies have been done on the nature of the difficulties in clergy marriage. One to which we have frequently referred is the one by David and Vera Mace on which they report in their book *What's Happening to Clergy Marriages?* Another is the one done by William B. Presnell and reported in his article "The Minister's Own Marriage," in *Pastoral Psychology*. Much of this chapter will be a reaction to the research of these studies, and others, and an incorporation of that material into the overall thrust of this book.

Presnell studied fifty-six clergy marriages and concluded that most clergy reduce their family roles to a minimum and have "difficulty in affirming their human needs, expressing their sexuality and . . . handling their anger openly."[8] I will look separately at each of these problem areas that Presnell has mentioned.

Clergy all too often minimize their family roles. Perhaps that is, in part, because so much emphasis has traditionally been put on their *professional* roles. The idea has been that if you are a minister of God, then all other roles should take a back seat. The church always comes first. And the church has a way of making more and more demands.

The results of this situation were shared by a minister from Oregon who wrote, "A strong sense of loyalty to the church, and guilt feelings about work undone, made my wife and children feel that they were third place (after God and church) in my life." An ex-wife from Washington State echoed similar thoughts, saying of her former husband, "He always put everyone with any need before his family. I got tired of taking second place to 'Mrs. Jones' and her difficulties."

When it comes to church programming, many accept the philosophy "The busier the better." And, of course, every program requires that the minister either leads it or at least is present to "show an interest" in what is happening. Here again the "Image" raises its ugly head. The superhuman minister is to lead all or lend his divine blessing to all. It's no wonder, then, that in a recent cross-denominational survey, when minister's wives were asked, "How many days have you had alone with your husband in the last month?" the response of over 50 percent of them was, "Not one."[9]

Sometimes this problem of overinvolvement in work becomes worse as a marriage deteriorates. Because the marriage is painful, the minister gets away from it by becoming more involved at church. One minister from Utah wrote, "Throwing myself at the job was one way of coping with a bad marriage that predated my coming to the church."

Whether the minister is becoming overinvolved in the church because the marriage is bad or because she is seeking to maintain the "Image," it is poor modeling for the rest of the congregation. Working sixty or seventy hours a week or more may help a minister maintain the "Image," and people may refer to the one who does so as a "selfless, tireless worker," working for Christ's glory. But doing this just validates the actions of other husbands or wives who feel their jobs are so important that they don't have time for their families.

Ministers who work sixty or seventy hours a week or more are not necessarily better ministers, either. Robert Pearse of Boston University has been quoted as saying that it is a myth that "the harder one works, the more he or she gets done." In reality, according to R. Alec MacKenzie, "executives who consistently devote more than forty-five to fifty hours a week to their jobs are in serious danger of impairing their efficiency. Several studies have shown that productivity declines rapidly after eight hours of work [per day]."[10] Michael LeBoeuf, professor of management, organizational behavior, and communications at the University of New Orleans, says that there is a big difference between being busy and being effective. He writes, "Many of us confuse activity with results. Yet, ironically, people have a tendency to be most busy when they are least confident in their abilities or goals."[11]

Ministers who are excessively busy are frequently that way because they refuse to delegate. Ministers need to trust their lay people with more work and decision-making. Part of a person's maturing in the faith has to include taking responsibility. Most lay people want to mature and to be able to decide and act without the pastor feeling she has to look over their shoulder all of the time.

Certainly, some churches want the minister there at every meeting. But if a congregation is concerned about their pastor's family, they need to support his right *not* to attend some meetings if his presence is not necessary.

Yet, in some churches it is true that the whole church is too busy. This not only tears the pastor from her family, but takes a lot of lay people from their families as well. In this regard, pastors and church boards need to look carefully at their programming so that it affirms the family by having activities in which families can participate together when possible and by making sure that any activity that requires people to be away from their families is well worth it.

Ministers then need to model the importance of family time. If a minister sees the prospect of spending time with his or her spouse as an unpleasant obligation, then he or she should seek professional counseling to confront the issue rather than running from it.

Presnell's work also mentioned the problem ministers have "affirming their human needs." This difficulty shows most evidently in the trouble ministers have receiving help and nurturing. But to recognize one's self as human is to recognize that one cannot stand alone as a self-sufficient "rock" on which others can always take refuge. Ministers must learn to share their needs and rely on others for help. They must do so, first of all, by learning to share with selected members of the congregation, or even the congregation as a whole, their humanness, their hurts, and their needs. Especially do they need to do so when their marriages are in trouble. Yet one of the most consistent responses I had from divorced ministers who responded to my questionnaire was that they had not let people in the congregation know their marriage was hurting until the time of separation or divorce. A Baptist minister from Washington wrote, "Ministry caused me to hide the problem from the congregations I served." A Methodist minister wrote, ". . . The congregation was not informed and, I learned later, was unaware of the difficulties and extent of the alienation. . . ." Another Baptist minister, who is now serving in a denominational position but who at the time was a pastor, wrote, "I am sure they were aware of difficulties but not aware of the severity of the marital problems."

Some ministers hesitate to share with the congregation because they feel it might "undermine their authority" with their people. There is the old "Image" again. To have authority the minister can't have weaknesses and needs. But a minister's authority can be enhanced when the people realize she is honest about her own shortcomings.

I realize that it is difficult for a minister to share his hurts with his congregation. In my own case, I had shared my marital struggles with a number of friends in the congregation for several years before my separation and divorce. But it was not always easy. And when I shared with the whole congregation that we were separating (a month before I decided to go ahead and file for divorce), it was very difficult. There is no way to share such a thing that is not awkward and uncomfortable. But the more people with whom I shared, the more I found that I was not destroyed by sharing my needs. It was good to find how supportive people can be.

Whether or not the minister can share with his congregation, he should most certainly find some trusted friends or colleagues with whom to share. Such people can serve as a support system. Some denominations encourage "clustering" of ministers for the purpose of fellowship and sharing. A minister does need to be selective, however, when it comes to choosing persons with whom to share personal information. One Baptist minister shared with me an incident in which a seminary professor mishandled some personal sharing by this minister's former spouse and caused a lot of guilt and pain that hurt the marriage. But this should not keep a person from sharing. There are certainly many competent, trustworthy people, and the need is great.

Other ministers need to be more open and caring towards such sharing. One minister from Washington, D.C., wrote of his experience prior to his divorce, "It was hard to find support among peers and I could not share with the congregation." In another case, a Baptist minister from the midwest wrote of marital stress that occurred when

So hard to say
        "I need"
So hard to say
            there are
            dark things
        inside me
            which I don't quite understand
            which scare me
        which are hard
            to let out
                into
                    the
                        Light.

Won't you
    shine
  your
    gentle
        understanding
    inside me
        and
            show me
        where
            to look?

his wife was undergoing a critical illness. He wrote, "We had no close friends, which we needed desperately." The difficulty of finding support and friendship from other ministers was also reported by at least one of the ministers interviewed by Mary LaGrand Bouma for her book *Divorce in the Parsonage*.[12] If ministers are to strengthen their marriages, they must band together to follow the biblical injunctions to "encourage one another."

Ministers must also affirm their needs by being open to receiving professional counseling. While the large majority of the ministers who responded to my questionnaire reported that they did go for marriage counseling, there are still some ministers who refuse or delay receiving such counseling because of professional pride. In the words of one pastor's ex-wife, ". . . ministers are often the last ones to feel or admit a need for counseling. They counsel *other* people. Frequently a minister's ego makes it extremely hard for him to seek help until it is too late."[13]

Denominations need to help encourage their ministers to go for such counseling, and many denominations are doing just that. The Maces found that one-half of the denominations they researched provide marriage counseling for clergy and two-thirds of them provide marriage enrichment experiences for ministers.[14] As denominations give help in these areas, it is important for denominational officials to heed the advice of Robert Stout and make it possible for ministers to go to a counselor who does *not* have a say in whether he or she is recommended to another church.[15] It is hard enough for ministers to go for counseling, without having the possibility that it might hurt their professional future looming overhead.

Ministers, then, need to model the truth that we all have needs and that we all need one another for support. If ministers can show that it is OK to have weaknesses, other people will find it easier to acknowledge their weaknesses.

Let us return now to Presnell's research on clergy marriage. A third area he mentioned in which ministers have difficulty is in "expressing their sexuality." Indeed, reports from many sources indicate that ministers are struggling in this area much more than most people would like to think. While it is doubtlessly true that most ministers behave sexually responsibly, reports of adultery, and other behavior indicating sexual confusion and unhappiness, abound. A newspaper article of

February 13, 1984, reported the story of a prominent Texas minister who was found beaten and strangled. Later investigation revealed he had been convicted and fined earlier for sex-related activities.

A recent story in *Leadership* magazine entitled ''The War Within: An Anatomy of Lust'' gives a frank account of one minister's personal struggle with pornography and how it had ruled his life for a long time. In sharing his struggle with other ministers, he found some who were having an even harder time with it.[16]

One former minister's wife reported to Mary LaGrand Bouma that during the time she was separated from her husband, three ministers offered to go to bed with her. According to Bouma, ''She said they actually assumed that they would be doing her a favor since she was no longer living with her husband. These were all married men.''[17]

Many cases are reported of male ministers becoming sexually involved with female counselees. Ann Bartram, who teaches pastoral counseling in the Toronto School of Theology, reports that in her own private practice at one point she was carrying a client load that included eight women, all of whom had had some kind of sexual relationship with the minister they were seeing for counseling.[18] While the subject of sexual involvement with counselees was not dealt with in my questionnaire, in my conversations with various persons and in the responses of a couple of former wives of ministers, I did run across a number of cases in which sexual involvement between a minister and a counselee was either suspected or else openly known and admitted.

There are several views of why so many male ministers are struggling in the area of sexual behavior. One writer relates it to the fact that the church is viewed as a ''feminine'' institution because it puts forth the traditionally feminine values of gentleness, nonviolence, and caring.[19] That these values are more acceptable to women is evidenced by the large percentage of women and small percentage of men in our churches. Male clergy who adhere to and teach such values may feel insecure about their manhood and feel the need to assert it. This also may explain why female clergy do not seem to be having as many problems with sexual involvements.

One minister's former wife believes that such adulterous relationships come about because ministers with weak egos feed on women with problems.[20] Put in a different way, ministers get much of their identity from a nurturing way of relating to people which, at its worst, can be

paternalistic and ego-serving; and which, when added to the vulnera-
bility of a woman in need, can easily be converted to a sexual involvement.

Robert Stout relates the problem to the fact that ministers are desirable
and prestigious targets for certain women. He writes, "There is little
doubt that there is a percentage of women who consider the sexual
conquest of a pastor a goal worth pursuing."[21]

Whatever the dynamics behind the sexual struggles of ministers,
these struggles must be seen as both causes and symptoms of marital
stress. They are causes of marital stress because few acts can disrupt
marital trust and intimacy to a greater degree than sexual infidelity.
They are symptoms of marital stress because when a relationship is
neglected or going bad, the sexual fulfillment of both partners suffers
and the partners are tempted to look elsewhere.

There are a number of ways a person might react to the difficulties
many clergy are having in their sexual lives. One can take the response
of cynicism and say, "Ministers are all a bunch of sexual hypocrites."
But this does not do justice to the majority of ministers who are acting
in sexually responsible ways, nor does it allow for the most helpful
approach to those who are having difficulty.

When my former wife and I were getting marriage counseling for
the first time at the Menninger Clinic in Topeka, the counselor told us
that his philosophy of counseling was this: "Everyone you meet is
doing the best he or she can with the resources available to him or
her." The task of counseling, then, is to help persons find new, more
helpful resources for dealing with their problems. Such resources could
be new understandings or new behaviors to help people grow and cope
with their environment. In this context, it needs to be understood that
ministers need additional resources to help them cope with their sexuality. As it is, their resources are limited, once again, by the "Image."
Because they try to live up to the flawless "Image" of what a minister
is supposed to be, they cannot admit that they are struggling with sexual
issues. This is aggravated by the fact that others assume ministers "have
it all together" in this area and don't need support. The result is that
ministers are limited to their own internal resources in combating sexual
temptation, whereas people in other professions can more readily seek
help from others.

The minister in such a situation can feel boxed in. If he wants to live up to the "Image," he can't admit the sexual difficulties, nor can he admit the marital problems that have caused or resulted from those difficulties. If he is boxed in long enough, he may risk an affair as a solution, gambling that it can be kept quiet, and the "Image" maintained.

Ministers need to be given other resources and options for dealing with such stress. They must have the option of counseling. In addition, ministers must have opportunities to talk over their own personal sexual problems, with one another or with a select number of others. But this will never happen as long as the minister is required to be seen as the kind of example who is above moral imperfection. The "Image" must fall.

In the context of these difficulties, when a minister does let the "Image" fall and does go for counseling or help, it is a real triumph. If the minister then goes on to divorce after facing these issues, the divorce can be seen as an attempt to regain legitimacy and find a more honest, straightforward solution to these sexual and personal problems.

Ministers, then, need to model the truth that we are all sexual creatures and that being sexual creatures is good, but they must face sexual tensions honestly, utilizing the support others can give.

The final point from Presnell's work that we will discuss is that ministers have trouble "handling their anger openly." David and Vera Mace underline this as an area of need, saying, "If the couples in our study are representative . . . half of all ministers and their wives are dissatisfied with their attempts to communicate effectively, to manage their negative feelings, and to resolve their conflicts successfully."[22] Anger also runs counter to the Image. Ministers are to be perfect examples of patience and control.

For a long time I bought the idea that I should avoid showing anger. But I began to learn, even sometime before my marriage ended, that I was paying a toll for such action. I was internalizing much of that anger. This brought about physical symptoms such as stomach problems and chest pains. In seminary I even thought I was having heart problems. But even worse than suffering these physical symptoms, I was denying my wife and others a chance to know who I really was, the good and the bad. Much of the anger was coming out in less direct and honest ways in my behavior. Counselors later pointed out to me that as I suppressed the anger, I also suppressed some of my caring and positive side as well.

People need permission to be human—to accept all of their feelings and express them. It takes such humanness to make good marriages. Ministers need to model this humanness by giving themselves permission to show anger in their marriages as well as in their other relationships.

While we have looked at all of the areas covered by Presnell's research, it would be inappropriate to conclude a discussion of modeling and clergy marriage without acknowledging that clergy should also model "sticking it out" when problems arise in marriage. The prophet Hosea did this in his marriage and used it to show how God does not give up on us in the midst of our rebellion. Love that does not care enough to fight for a marriage in the midst of problems is not love in the biblical sense. However, this does not mean that patience with a bad marriage must go on indefinitely. While our patience should *point to* God's, it should not necessarily be expected to *equal* God's. There comes a time when even God says, "No more!"

Certainly, as we mentioned in the last chapter, the divorced ministers who responded to my query showed every evidence of having stuck with problem relationships for a long time, trying to work out solutions. And that is the way it should be.

Ministers, then, need to model what it takes to make marriage work. This means facing up to all kinds of weaknessess and needs. It means giving a high priority to family. And it means having a high commitment to work through problems. As with any human being, ministers will not always be successful models. But with the support and understanding of their churches and with a new commitment on the part of the ministers to face this challenge with an openness to voice their needs and receive help from others, ministers will be able to do a far better job of modeling what God wants in marriage.

Some Biblical Perspectives on Divorce

Some people may object and say that while it is true that ministers cannot be perfect and that ministers who remain married may also come up short in modeling what God wants in marriage, divorce is still contrary to what the Bible says. They believe that a person who deliberately decides for a divorce is acting in willful disobedience to God and hence is not worthy of being a minister. After all, it's one thing to have weaknesses and still another to be willfully disobedient.

Because of feelings such as these, it is important that we look at some biblical perspectives on divorce. However, we need to do more than just look at Scriptures relating to divorce. How we apply the Bible to the question of divorce is inseparably related to our understanding of the relative roles of law and grace.

Christians today have really not come to terms with some of the tension between law and grace. We know that Jesus opposed a legalistic approach and that he came to show God's grace. But we tend to fear that too much emphasis on grace will result in people believing that everything is morally OK because we are no longer under the law. This fear is at least as old as the New Testament, because Paul dealt with it extensively.

It's not that some Christians believe in law and some in grace. Rather, Christians differ about the relative roles of each. Some believe that grace only means that if we fall short of what the law says, we will be forgiven; but law is still the criterion by which we judge whether certain behaviors are permissible. Others believe that grace also has implications for how Christians live their lives and that Christian behavior cannot be reduced to laws. If one has the former viewpoint, then divorce is blatant disobedience. Hence, while divorce is a forgivable sin, it is most definitely wrong. But if the latter view is taken, then such a black-and-white judgment cannot be made. It is my contention that the latter view has the most scriptural support and allows for a more clear delineation between the Christian faith and legalistic religion.

The issue of the roles of law and grace is not simple. Paul used most of his letters to the Romans and to the Galatians to try to explain the relationship, and many think he still never made it clear. But if Paul thought that our moral guide is still the law and that the only change is that now we are forgiven when we fail, it would have been very simple for him to say that clearly. What is more, he would have had little reason for contention with those who opposed him. Even Judaism taught that God is merciful and will graciously forgive.

So while the issues of law and grace are not simple, I will summarize, as clearly as possible, how I see the biblical position. The Bible's position is this: (1) The sole function of law is to show our need for grace; (2) grace is the prescription for our spiritual illness, which the law has made manifest; and (3) the Spirit (and the love that is part of life in the Spirit), and *not* the law, is our present moral guide.

1. The fact that the function of law is to show our need for grace is asserted by Paul in the seventh chapter of Romans. He says in verses 6 and 7:

> But now we have been released from the Law, having died to that by which we were bound, so that we serve in newness of the Spirit and not in the oldness of the letter.
> What shall we say then? Is the Law sin? May it never be! On the contrary, I would not have come to know sin except through the Law; for I would not have known about coveting if the Law had not said, ''You shall not covet.''

Thus the law shows what the ideal is, what God wants everyone to attain. But in actual experience, the sinful nature of people is only made more evident by the law. And the more we are aware of what we are supposed to do, the more we do the opposite when the law is our only resource. By itself, the law frustrates and enslaves us because we cannot come near to filling its demands. It is necessary only because apart from the law we would be living in ignorance, assuming that what we do and are is pleasing to God. The law shows us that there is an illness, but it gives no cure.

2. The prescription for our illness is God's grace. While the law seemingly joins forces with our sinful nature to enslave us, Paul tells us in Romans 6:14 that "sin shall not be master over you, for you are not under the Law, but under grace." Paul is even more specific in Ephesians 2:8-9 when he says, "For by grace you have been saved through faith; and that not of yourselves, it is the gift of God; not as a result of works, that no one should boast."

But we can retain this freedom only if we rely *solely* on grace for our status before God. If we want to gain status through the law, then we have to obey the whole law. Thus Paul says in Galatians 5:1-3:

> It was for freedom that Christ set us free; therefore keep standing firm and do not be subject again to a yoke of slavery. Behold I, Paul, say to you that if you receive circumcision, Christ will be of no benefit to you. And I testify again to every man who receives circumcision, that he is under obligation to keep the whole Law.

The clear implication is that those who *do* rely solely on grace through Jesus Christ are *not* obligated to "keep the whole Law."

Some would say that Christ frees us only from the Jewish ceremonial law and that we remain obligated to keep the part of the law which deals with personal morality. But Paul clearly says here that once we start relying on *any* part of the law, you are obligated to keep *all* of it. Furthermore, the previously mentioned passage in Romans 7:6-7 specifically refers to our freedom from the law that says, "Do not covet."

3. Because Paul took the position he did on salvation by grace through faith, he had to show how such a view did not encourage people to live immoral, irresponsible lives. Again, if he believed that even though we are saved by God's grace, we should still live according to the law's dictates as best we can, he could have said that clearly and concisely. And he would not have brought upon himself the opposition of Judaistic Christianity. But an important part of grace for Paul was that it gives us a different moral guide. He refers to this new moral guide in Romans 8:2: "For the law of the Spirit of life in Christ Jesus has set you free from the law of sin and of death." This "law of the Spirit of life in Christ Jesus" is not a new legalism but, rather, is simply the act of letting the Holy Spirit guide us. This is said well in Romans 7:6: "But now we have been released from the Law . . . so that we serve in

newness of the Spirit and not in oldness of the letter."

For those who are uncomfortable with such lack of structure, living by the Spirit's leading is not totally unstructured. Paul makes it clear that the Spirit guides us to act in love. Thus he writes in Romans 13:8-10:

> Owe nothing to anyone except to love one another; for he who loves his neighbor has fulfilled the law. For this, "You shall not commit adultery, You shall not murder, You shall not steal, You shall not covet," and if there is any other commandment, it is summed up in this saying, "You shall love your neighbor as yourself." Love does no wrong to a neighbor; love is therefore the fulfillment of the law.

To walk in the Spirit is to realize, then, that the letter of the law needs to be superseded by the dictates of love. This is what Jesus also taught when he healed and met people's needs on the sabbath. "The Sabbath was made for man, and not man for the Sabbath." "Right" and "wrong" still exist, but the distinction is that they are based on love rather than on rigid law.

Because we no longer are under law, the main criterion for our behavior is what is helpful to our growth and the growth of others. Thus Paul says in 1 Corinthians 6:12, "All things are lawful for me, but not all things are profitable. All things are lawful for me, but I will not be mastered by anything." Some behaviors enslave us to our passions and these are not "profitable" for our growing. Some behaviors hurt other people and these are not "profitable" for their growing.

Admittedly, there are some sayings of Christ that could be interpreted as being counter to what we have said. Christ says in Matthew 5:17, "Do not think that I came to abolish the Law and the Prophets; I did not come to abolish, but to fulfill." However, if this is understood in the context of Paul's statement that "love . . . is the fulfillment of the law," then certainly Christ came to fulfill the law. He fulfilled it by bringing the love and grace that the law showed was needed. But he also came to start a new era. He says in Luke 16:16, "The Law and the Prophets were proclaimed until John; since then the gospel of the kingdom of God is preached. . . ."

Christ also says in Matthew 5:18-19:

> "For truly I say to you, until heaven and earth pass away, not the smallest letter or stroke shall pass away from the Law, until all is accomplished. Whoever then annuls one of the least of these commandments, and so teaches others, shall be called least in the kingdom of heaven; but

whoever keeps and teaches them, he shall be called great in the kingdom of heaven.''

This verse is an even more problematic saying than the verse that preceded it. Some say this passage was in reality either created by Matthew or heavily edited by him.[1] The only part that is included in the other Gospels is a variation of verse 18, which shows up in Luke 16:17; but here it sounds more like a sarcastic reference to the resistance of the Pharisees when Christ attempted to humanize the law. It can also be pointed out that Matthew had a high regard for Jewish tradition and observance, and so such editing could have been done to make Christ's sayings more in line with his own thinking. Nonetheless, the saying cannot be dismissed. Traditionally it has been accepted as a saying of Jesus, and we cannot prove conclusively that it is otherwise. Even if we could do so, it is still part of our New Testament Scripture.

While these verses cannot simply be dismissed, I would agree with what George Buttrick says in *The Interpreter's Bible*: ''. . . The best commentary on their meaning is found in the whole life and teaching of Jesus.''[2] Jesus consistently resisted the legalistic approach of the Pharisees. He himself overruled commandments on sabbath observance, ceremonial cleansing, and punishment of adultery. What needs to be said, as an implication of the New Testament as a whole, is that while *people* do not have the authority to annul the law, *God* has made it obsolete by virtue of the act of redemption in Jesus Christ.

The Christian, then, is to live as led by the Spirit, which is flexible to human need, and not by the inflexible law. It is rather like the *Star Wars* movie when Luke Skywalker elected to be guided by ''The Force'' rather than by his computer.

What, then, are the implications of this understanding of grace for the issue of divorce? To determine this, let's look at some of the New Testament Scriptures that refer specifically to divorce.

First of all, Jesus says in Matthew 5:31-32:

> ''And it was said, 'Whoever divorces his wife, let him give her a certificate of dismissal'; but I say to you that every one who divorces his wife, except for the cause of unchastity, makes her commit adultery; and whoever marries a divorced woman commits adultery.''

This verse must be seen in the context of both the view of law and grace previously discussed and the verses which immediately surround it. In the verses which precede and follow, we are told that the one who hates a brother or sister is the same as a murderer, that lusting after another person is the same as committing adultery, and that if one's eye or hand causes one to sin, the offending member should be cut out rather than allowed to continue to lead one in sin. The passage on divorce cannot be isolated from these verses and dealt with differently. If we are to be bound by the divorce passage as law, then we also must be bound by the other passages. To consider these passages as law would leave every Christian maimed and probably having to consider himself or herself a murderer or an adulterer, or both. Is that what Jesus meant by Good News?

To place such a tremendous moral burden on people would be weighing them down worse than the Pharisees did, and of the Pharisees Jesus said in Matthew 23:4, "They tie up heavy loads, and lay them on men's shoulders; but they themselves are unwilling to move them with so much as a finger."

It is more appropriate to see all of these verses in the light of what Paul said about the purpose of the law being to show how hopelessly mired we are in sin. The Pharisees thought they had the moral strength to live up to the law. But they were able to think so only because they did not realize how truly demanding the law is. This is why Jesus said in Matthew 5:20, "Unless your righteousness surpasses that of the scribes and Pharisees, you shall not enter the kingdom of heaven." When we truly realize how demanding the law is we also realize that on the basis of law, none can stand.

In a more extended treatment of divorce, we read in Matthew 19:3-9:

> And some Pharisees came to Him, testing Him, and saying, "Is it lawful for a man to divorce his wife for any cause at all?" And He answered and said, "Have you not read, that He who created them from the beginning made them male and female, and said, 'For this cause a man shall leave his father and mother, and shall cleave to his wife; and the two shall become one flesh'? Consequently they are no more two, but one flesh. What therefore God has joined together, let no man separate."
> They said to Him, "Why then did Moses command to give her a certificate and divorce her?"
> He said to them, "Because of your hardness of heart, Moses permitted you to divorce your wives; but from the beginning it has not been this way. And I say to you, whoever divorces his wife, except for immorality, and marries another commits adultery."

This is a complicated passage, so we can approach it best by looking at key passages. Christ says it is not "lawful" to divorce because of the principle contained in the Scripture ". . . and the two shall become one flesh." But an important question is, Does this mean Christ says we must not divorce? Or does it mean that divorce is not consistent with the ideal that God envisioned for us "from the beginning," that is, not in accord with the law? Obviously, divorce was not any more in accord with the law in Old Testament times, but God "permitted" it. There are then two issues: "What is lawful?" and "What is permitted?"

If we ask, "Is divorce lawful?" the answer is evidently, "No." It is not in accord with the ideal God has envisioned from the beginning, which is expressed in the law. But if we ask, "Is divorce permitted?", we are dealing with a different issue. To say that God permitted divorce in the Old Testament because God knew of the imperfections of people but that God won't permit divorce now, is to say that when dealing with the issue of divorce (and seemingly with this issue alone), God was more gracious in Old Testament times than God is now. In point of fact, Christ did not expressly say that divorce was no longer permitted. More specifically, he only said why it is not in accord with the law— "from the beginning it was not so."

That Christ would have championed human need over against sabbath laws and not have done the same in regard to divorce laws seems inconsistent at best. I would agree with Larry Richards who writes, "If in the Old Testament God permitted divorce, and built that provision into Scripture's revelation of his will, it can only be because at times there can be greater hurt, greater damage to persons, by remaining married than by divorcing."[3]

Christ was really objecting to the way the Pharisees took what was a gracious permission and turned it into part of the law, the ideal. Thus, Pharisees who divorced could still see themselves as living in accord with the law when they were not.

This latter point is also behind what Christ was saying in the statement, "What therefore God has joined together, let no man separate." If it is God who joins, then God alone has the right to separate. The Pharisees had "bent" the law a little to include this gracious permission. In doing so, they were taking upon themselves to declare something "lawful" that God had declared "unlawful." They were giving themselves the right to separate what God had joined.

It is God who graciously permits divorce—not because it is in accord with law, but because it is God's right as the Bestower of grace.

God is part of the joining of two people in marriage. People make the decision to marry. But in Christian marriage they should seek God's guidance on that decision. Whether they do or not, God's blessing is part of the joining together. In the same respect, because God graciously permits divorce, God should also be part of the decision-making process in divorce. It is not only perfectly legitimate to seek God's guidance in a divorce decision, it is vital for the Christian. If God is part of the joining together, God must also be given a part in the separating.

What then about the passage "Whoever divorces his wife, except for immorality, and marries another commits adultery"? This is a restatement of a similar saying in Matthew 5:32. It is significant to note that the parallel verses in the other Gospels do not even allow the "except for immorality" provision. Matthew again may have inserted this phrase to keep the saying more in line with Jewish tradition.

We need to see this teaching once again in context: when judged by the law as ideal, even those who lust after someone other than their spouse are adulterers. Under the law there are none who do not stand as adulterers, murderers, false witnesses, or some other equally sinful status. That's why grace is so important.

Before leaving this Scripture, we need also to look at the phrase "The two shall become one flesh." This is the ideal of marriage in a positive form. Marriage is to be a unity in which intimacy can be found in a way unequaled in any other human relationship. As Gary Demarest has written, "Marriage is designed by God to be a lifelong relationship in which a woman and a man grow into each other as in no other human relationship."[4] The process of "growing into each other" is not without times when growth is set back or arrested. But growth should occur. A marriage that does not have this oneness is already short of what God calls marriage to be. And if, in spite of all efforts, growth toward oneness does not occur, then divorce is only the recognition of falling short of the ideal.

Christ's priority of love needs also to be applied to these verses. He put human need over law and told us that the first items on our agenda should be love of God and love of our neighbors as ourselves. Divorce can be anti-love. In Christ's time some rabbis taught that a person could divorce his wife on the basis of even the smallest imperfection. Women who were divorced in that society were really out on a limb because they had virtually no way to support themselves. To divorce over small issues because some rabbi said it was "lawful" was quite unloving. And certainly this kind of divorce happens today. Even a divorce that occurs because of an incident of infidelity, grounds that at least Matthew may have viewed as "lawful," can be vindictive and unloving if no attempt is made at forgiveness and reconciliation.

If the patterns of a marriage are such that even after all attempts at healing the marriage is only destructive to both partners, it is unloving to place their hurt and pain as of secondary importance to law. It is a legitimate paraphrase of Christ's words to say, "The law was made for people, and not people for the law."

An important passage from Paul on divorce can be found in 1 Corinthians 7:10-15. In this passage we read:

> But to the married I give instructions, not I, but the Lord, that the wife should not leave her husband (but if she does leave, let her remain unmarried, or else be reconciled to her husband), and that the husband should not send his wife away.
>
> But to the rest I say, not the Lord, that if any brother has a wife who is an unbeliever, and she consents to live with him, let him not send her away. And a woman who has an unbelieving husband, and he consents to live with her, let her not send her husband away. For the unbelieving husband is sanctified through his wife, and the unbelieving wife is sanctified through her believing husband; for otherwise your children are unclean, but now they are holy.
>
> Yet if the unbelieving one leaves, let him leave; the brother or sister is not under bondage in such cases, but God has called us to peace.

Most certainly we need to look at this passage in the light of Paul's overall view of law and grace, which we have already discussed. The one who declared us "free from the law" is not about to burden us with laws of his own. This is evident from the absence of legalistic language. In these "instructions" he makes provision for those who choose to do other than what he advises ("but if she does . . .").

This passage should be seen in the context of what Paul says in the chapter just before this one: "All things are lawful for me, but not all things are profitable." He does not see divorce as helpful in light of the attempts of Christians to build a witness in Corinth. Sticking with an unbelieving spouse could be a positive witness to Christ in this unbelieving city.

Certainly what Paul says has implications for our time as well. We need to be mindful of our total lifestyle and how it affects our witness. Divorce among Christians, especially Christian ministers, can hurt our witness. This is especially true if our behavior indicates to others that we are irresponsible in our task of doing all we can to nurture love in marriage. But poor marriages, laced with falsehood, are just as bad for our witness, if not worse. The non-Christian who sees us doing our best to face marital problems responsibly and honestly will in most cases be favorably affected.

The fact that these verses from Paul are "instructions" concerning what he viewed as "profitable" for the Christians of this time means we need not take them in a legalistic way. Rather, we should take them as part of the input we need as the Spirit leads us in determining what is profitable for our own spiritual growth.

Grace is the key to how we look at divorce. It should then not be surprising to learn that when I asked divorced ministers in my questionnaire, "How does your divorce fit into your present theological perspective?" a great number of them referred to their new appreciation of the meaning of grace. Grace was not just an intellectual issue or a question of biblical interpretation. It had become an experiential reality. A Baptist minister wrote, "My divorce afforded me the opportunity to experience God's grace in its fullness. I was able to extend to myself the love and forgiveness and acceptance I have previously given to others . . . over the years." And a minister now serving a special appointment in Oregon wrote, ". . . When it happened, God sent healing (a real sign to me of God's presence) and forgiveness."

In my own case, my remarriage has especially been evidence to me of God's continuing grace in my life. When I was struggling in my first marriage, the "little child" inside of me withdrew into a shell to avoid being hurt. My new wife, Cathy, has drawn that "child" out of me again. She has helped my wounds to heal and has helped make my life exciting and fulfilling once again. God has been gracious to me through her. I know by my experience, as well as God's promises, that God is with me.

That God gives such grace does not make divorce "lawful" or even good. Divorce will never be in line with what God ultimately wants. But the sin is not in the action of divorce. It is in the weakness, the "hardness of heart," which turns a marriage bad. And as I know the reality of God's grace, I also confess that I am aware of many times when my sinfulness brought pain and destruction to my previous marriage. But fighting sin's effect on marriage is not done by disallowing divorce but by working continually to keep sin from destroying marriage in the first place. Divorce is but an outward confession of what sin has done. And the Bible calls us toward confession.

The People Mourn— The People Support

Whenever divorce occurs, it is never just an individual issue. It is also a community issue. The pain that divides the couple also cuts into and divides the church community. This is especially so when a minister is involved. The minister and spouse are like family to many church people. The divorce of a minister is a church-family issue.

Because the congregation and other church people are like family, the divorce of the minister causes strain for them for some time to come. Mike Fitzgibbons, an Episcopal priest from Washington State, has twice served in parishes immediately following a predecessor who was divorced. He has pointed out to me that the congregation goes through the same process of mourning that the minister and his or her ex-spouse go through. The mourning process is similar to that which Elizabeth Kübler-Ross says a person goes through when someone close dies.[1] While such a mourning process cannot be totally reduced to an orderly process, Kübler-Ross lists five stages that Mike Fitzgibbons says can also be seen in congregations mourning the divorce of a minister.

1. *Denial.* Denial is most certainly present in the time immediately preceding the announcement of a divorce. Fitzgibbons noted that "people notice and do not pay attention to the recognition that the pastor and his wife are having trouble. . . ." They selectively don't hear the danger signals given off in a troubled marriage. Fitzgibbons went on to tell me, "The ones who sense the most first tend to keep the secret, protecting their clergyman and spouse. . . ."

A situation in which denial may have occurred was described for me by a Baptist minister from New Jersey who wrote in regard to her situation, "When they figured out that I had left my husband and intended to file for divorce, they were shocked at first, but then they began to look back and realize how certain things fit together (things that they had just chalked up to eccentricity on my part or my husband's part)." She went on to say, "I think that they were embarrassed that they hadn't figured out what was going on long before they did, especially since there were plenty of signs."

This denial carries over frequently to the time after the divorce announcement. At this point denial shows up in the form of shock and the inability to believe it is really going to happen. This phenomenon was reported by several divorced ministers who responded to my questionnaire. Along with the shock came confusion about what to do and how to respond. The divorce of a minister is not something for which congregations are prepared. It is therefore understandable that most react with denial and feelings of confusion. I hope that this book will help bring greater understanding and direction to such churches.

2. *Bargaining.* Mike Fitzgibbons believes that in this stage the congregation believes that if, in a somewhat mythical way, they can just be a better congregation and pray more to God, God will keep the divorce from happening and will bring the couple back together again. This is similar to the kind of reaction people have noted in children when there is an impending divorce or death.

3. *Anger.* This stage can be expressed in people's withdrawal from church, either physically or financially or both. It can also be expressed in church members taking sides and blaming. In my own case, there was a very strong tendency for people in the church to feel the need to take sides. Some people who were formerly friends of both my former wife and myself found it difficult to maintain a position of being friends to both of us after the divorce. They felt a definite need to take sides and place the blame. Some took one side and some took the other. But the need to choose and to blame *someone* seems to be related to the people's need to express their anger that the divorce occurred at all.

Anger in this situation is real and needs to be expressed by all persons involved, including the congregation. But if there was friendship with both parties before the divorce, it would seem healthier and more honest to express anger *and* support to both parties after the divorce.

4. *Depression*. This stage is evidenced by activities that lack zest and by people who drop out. Depression is a natural reaction to a situation that is painful, especially when there is no obvious plan of action to alleviate the pain. Pain combined with confusion of direction is an invitation to depression. This could be alleviated if denominational officials and church leaders could help the people express their feelings in a constructive way (much as a counselor does with a client) and help them think through implications for their ministry as a congregation. Certainly this process cannot always be done easily, especially in denominations where there is high congregational autonomy. But congregations need to be helped to understand that working through feelings and finding a sense of direction is an essential part of recovering from a minister's divorce and reaffirming their ministry as a church.

5. *Acceptance*. This is the stage in which' the congregation has accepted what has occurred by working through feelings and is ready to go on with ministry. Mike Fitzgibbons notes that, in instances in which the divorced minister leaves, this stage may or may not occur before the next minister is called. He asserts that "selecting a new clergyperson may be a means of not dealing with the loss." This approach can lead to future problems, in the same way it does in a remarriage when the loss of a previous spouse has not been dealt with adequately.

William Bridges, in his book *Transitions*, points out that one should not rush through the transitions of life. A person needs to deal emotionally with the "endings" of one life situation, and then have a "neutral" transitional time before going on to new "beginnings."[2] Rushing that process by not dealing emotionally with the endings can only bring adjustment problems as one seeks new beginnings. This is true for groups of people, like congregations, as well as for individuals. Persons who have not dealt with the emotions of the endings that occur when a minister divorces and leaves—emotions such as anger and guilt—will only have those feelings disrupt their relationship with the new minister.

Still, I am convinced that in most situations the best course of all is for the divorced minister not to leave at all. Mourning is best done when all parties involved can work through feelings together.

When a person dies, the loved one who remains must work through many feelings. He has to deal with guilt about ways he has hurt the person who died. He has to deal with anger about the other person "leaving" him. He needs to express his love. If the person dies suddenly, and hence is not present to be part of the sharing of feelings, it is much more difficult for the survivor than if the person is known to be dying for some time. When there is time for the dying person and loved ones to share feelings, those feelings are more likely to be worked through. Dealing with those feelings together can produce a time of real intimacy.

When a minister divorces, her congregation also has to work through many feelings, as we have already noted. If the minister leaves right away, the people are robbed of the chance of working through those feelings with the person who has been their minister and finding together the intimacy that can result.

What are other factors that influence how well a congregation works through its mourning? Mike Fitzgibbons sees a number of factors at work in this process. First of all, there is the life history of the members and how they have experienced and dealt with other losses. As I see this factor operating, I am aware that people tend to deal with all losses in their lives in a similar manner. If they have dealt with previous loss principally by withdrawal, they will withdraw when the minister is divorced. If they have dealt with previous loss principally by striking out in anger, they will probably do that when the minister is divorced. Also relevant here is whether or not they have had to experience the loss of divorce in their own family. If they have, they generally are more tolerant of the minister's divorce when they have indeed worked through their feelings about divorce. If they have not worked through those feelings, they may have some residual anger to dump on the minister or former spouse.

A second factor Fitzgibbons sees is how ecclesiastical authorities respond. Are they helping people to work through feelings or do they fan the flames with their own anger that the minister has stepped out of the Image?

A third factor is how well or how poorly the minister and spouse handle their own processes. Congregations have a hard time accepting divorce if it becomes apparent that an affair by the minister was part of the situation. Also, if the minister and spouse turn their divorce into a public battle, enlisting members in the fight, it produces a terrible strain on the church.

The final factor listed by Fitzgibbons is the sense of blame the congregation puts on themselves as "children" in the family. In a divorce situation children frequently blame themselves for their parents' divorce. Since the congregation members are like their pastor's spiritual children, this same process can happen in ministerial divorce. One minister told me how this had been in his situation. The minister who had preceded him had been divorced while serving the congregation. When he also was divorced while serving the same congregation, the people were definitely asking, "What are we doing wrong?" Part of the congregation's mourning has to include working through this feeling of guilt, which is not necessarily appropriate guilt.

A factor I would add to those Mike Fitzgibbons suggested is how close the congregation has become to the minister and spouse. In one case the minister told me that the congregation had not really become very close to his former spouse (that had been a problem in the marriage), and so when they divorced and she left, they did not really have the sense of loss they might have had. On the other hand, if the congregation feels distant from the minister, a divorce may bring the anger about this fact to the surface; the congregation may be more likely to deal with him as a "divorced minister" than as a person who is hurting.

In the midst of the congregation's mourning, how do the members then act toward the minister? Certainly in some cases there is ultimate rejection. A Presbyterian minister wrote that in his case two elders out of six were supportive, three were noncommittal and one (together with his wife) was very vocal in opposition. In response, the minister took a leave of absence and then resigned after two months. The minister, whose divorce was final just prior to this writing, went on to say, "The church never even said, 'Thank you' nor did they make any official communication in any way for my five-plus years of ministry to them."

It should be noted that in this case a vocal minority opposition spelled the pastor's doom. In the cases reported to me in which the minister resigned, this was the rule rather than the exception. In such situations, the minister feels he must make a choice. A minister from western Washington wrote of how he made his: "I resigned because if I had stayed, I'd have polarized the congregation."

The issue of polarization in the congregation needs to be looked at more carefully. Mike Fitzgibbons, in his communication with me, pointed to other factors at work. He wrote, "The matter of polarization is—I believe—rarely the fault of the clerical divorce, though this might bring such a matter to a head. That is, unless the divorce occurs remarkably soon after the pastor assumes a pastorate, the clergyperson has usually done (or not done) things or has trod on someone's coattails. So the issue is rarely, I believe, as clean as it is often portrayed." In the case of the minister from Washington, this was just the case. He noted that there was a group already wanting to "get him" previous to his divorce, and the divorce just gave them ammunition.

Ministers and congregational leadership who face the possibility of a polarized congregation because of the minister's divorce, need to take a hard look at the nature and value of conflict. Certainly, nobody likes to be the center of an angry debate threatening the harmony of the church. But can the church truly minister in today's world while maintaining a principle of "peace and harmony at all costs"? The church that avoids conflict must avoid the most vital issues of life! Certainly there are times when the conflict is not worth the cost. But church communities that face conflict and work through it can achieve a new intimacy and understanding they will never have if they always avoid conflict. Furthermore, they will be establishing a precedent for dealing with future conflict.

Ministers who work in other than church pastorates can also face opposition upon their divorce. A minister serving in a hospital chaplaincy in the midwest wrote, "There was one hospital administrator of very conservative stance who wanted me fired, but I got good support from the department chairman and survived."

When clergy divorce results in the minister losing his or her position, it is tragic. It compounds pain with more pain. In cases in which the minister has shown poor moral judgment, the ending of employment may be necessary. But in most cases needless hurt is done. One minister's former wife described the situation with great empathy when she wrote: "I have observed one situation in which there was a clergy divorce. Both were asked to leave the parsonage; the clergy spouse was asked to leave the job. What an emotional/psychological trauma! As if divorce weren't enough loss and pain, you have to add to it the loss of your home or your job! Then if older children are forced to choose sides, one spouse may lose the children, too. Wow!" Congregations and denominational leaders need to be aware of this pain and trauma when decisions are made.

The congregation will mourn. It may even experience some divisiveness. But the minister's divorce may also provide an opportunity for a congregation to give emotional support to the pastor instead of vice versa, hence making the relationship more total and genuine. Most pastors, as part of the "Image" of strength and perfection by which they seek to live, are far more comfortable giving help than receiving it. When a pastor is divorced and experiences the tremendous need and pain that accompany divorce, this must change. And if the change brings mutual giving and receiving, the pastor-church relationship will be enhanced.

The good news of the survey I took was that the large majority of ministers who responded felt supported by the people with whom they ministered. Of those in pastorates, twenty-six of the thirty-four ministers who responded said that their congregations were either mostly or totally supportive of them. And those in institutional or counseling work only rarely encountered people who were critical or judgmental.

While the ministers who responded felt supported by people of all groups, several mentioned particularly the support they received from other divorced people. A campus minister from Oregon wrote, "Persons who had gone through divorce themselves readily came to me to share their own experiences. . . ." An Episcopal minister wrote, "Several lay people who had been divorced reached out to me, and families have sought to include me in holiday and other activities." One minister noted that while most people showed concern about how he was, there was a difference in sensitivity between those who had never been divorced and those who had. Those who had never been divorced frequently asked personal questions at the church door after the service, a place where an honest response could be awkward. Those who had been divorced realized this, and asked in private, when the pastor could give an honest and more detailed response.

But support is certainly felt from many groups of people, not just those who have been divorced. A minister from Washington, D.C., wrote that the men of the church formed an "unofficial support group" around him. They invited him to their homes and visited him in his apartment. A Methodist minister noted that he had many more dinner invitations after his divorce. He also noted that in a new congregation he was pastoring, a "couples' club" was changed to the "adult fellowship" in order to include him and other single adults. A minister from Massachusetts wrote that the people of her congregation were careful to check and see that she was not alone on holidays.

Sometimes the support comes from former congregations, as well from as the present one. A minister from New Jersey reported that members of her former church frequently call or visit. She went on to note, "People who I thought were not that supportive, call me and check up on how I'm doing."

When I was divorced, I was concerned about how my former church in Wamego, Kansas, might react. I knew I could not go back to everyone and explain my thoughts and feelings. But their reactions were important to me because they were my friends. It was a healing experience when several wrote me and, while expressing their sadness, also expressed their support of both me and my former wife. Two families invited me to join them for dinner on one occasion at one of their homes. I was nervous that I was going to be "on the spot" or need to defend my position. But it was not that way at all. They wanted to know my feelings. They wanted to know how I was doing spiritually in the midst of everything. They did not judge. I shared, in tears, the agony I had gone through in making the decision, and they listened. Their words and their hugs lifted me.

Later when my new wife, my stepdaughter, and I were on our way to our new church in Oakesdale, these families invited us to stop by. They had invited several other families from the church, and we found that being in touch with them was an invigorating boost for us on our way into our new future.

Ministers mentioned many general ways of showing support: prayers, cooperation, budget help, hugs, words of encouragement, and so forth. But there were also some specific, concrete acts that were central for some ministers. Since, as I mentioned before, there is a tendency for a minister to resign when divorced (in order to avoid polarization within the congregation), it was important to a minister from Washington that one of the first things his board did was to ask him specifically *not* to resign. They didn't even want him to consider it. When a U.C.C. minister from New York did resign, the church in its annual meeting refused the resignation. Such actions affirm a person's ministry and speak well of the character of the congregations involved.

One divorced minister, a personal friend of mine, told me that one way his church has shown support of him has been by encouraging his dating. Some have given him names of single women in whom they thought he might be interested. This encouragement is particularly important, since some church people might not be comfortable with their minister dating. It could be thought of as "not spiritual."

The other side of the dating issue, however, is that some people, by encouraging the minister to date, may be saying that they are not comfortable with the minister being single. A minister from Massachusetts wrote that she felt the church people were being supportive by not attempting to "fix her up" or saying, "You should be married." Support for dating can mean different things to different people, and apparently in both of these situations the churches were supportive because they were sensitive to where their respective ministers were on the subject of dating.

A minister from New Jersey wrote that one way her church was supportive was in providing prompt help with repairs around the parsonage. Such help is of particular importance if a person is alone and is not mechanically inclined.

An important area in which I have received support has been my children. While I have joint custody of my daughters, Angela and Carina, their mother has primary residence. When we were divorced, a principal area of anxiety for me was how often I was going to be able to see my children if I moved away. I have always been close to my children, but I knew that ministers cannot always find a church in the area of the country they prefer. After I had explored several possibilities in Kansas that did not work out, I was contacted by the church in Oakesdale, Washington. My new wife, Cathy, and I visited with the people several times, and the church seemed to be one where we could feel comfortable. But there was still the issue of my children. Oakesdale is seventeen hundred miles from their home in Topeka! I shared my feelings with the pulpit committee, and after some discussion among themselves they decided to set up a special fund over and above my salary to fly my daughters to nearby Spokane. They called the fund the "H.K. Fund," which was to stand for either the "Hugs and Kisses Fund" or "His Kids' Fund"! The concern they expressed in this way confirmed to us that this was where we belonged.

Perhaps the most vital support of all is emotional support, especially (but not exclusively) during the time immediately following the divorce. Many ministers wrote about receiving this kind of support. But perhaps the most moving example was provided me by a minister from Oregon. One experience of his was so exciting that I will quote him in full. He wrote:

> Two weeks after my wife had said finally, "I'm never coming back" (she had been away at school for six months, but I'd still been hoping for reconciliation), I went to a previously scheduled "Serendipity Workshop" with Lyman Coleman. His theme was "Frog Kissing." I went feeling very much as if I had been changed into an ugly, wart-covered, rejected web-footed amphibian. At the end of a full day of personal sharing and affirming experiences, each person was invited to share with his small group his greatest need. In my group I went first—"I need God's help to overcome bitterness and to learn to be effective as a divorced minister." Another minister in the group expressed his empathy, and each one prayed for me. Then the next step was for the person to be affirmed and commissioned by the group. I lay on my back and the other seven picked me up and gently supported and rocked me—the loving, tender support I wanted so much. The member nearest me, a little Catholic nun called "Sister Rosie," then placed a Jerusalem cross medallion around my neck and kissed me on the cheek! We then went on to each other person in the group.
>
> Three days later, I was writing my sister and two brothers about the end of my marriage. Having shared the sad news, I wanted to find something better to say and I related the story above. As I wrote the words about bitterness, I stopped to realize, "Hey—I don't feel bitter toward her (my wife) any more! Praise the Lord!" After three days resurrection had taken place—and I felt as though the ugly old frog might become at least a forgiven human being, if not a prince, once more."

When a minister experiences emotional support in such a beautiful way as this, it can touch his life in two ways. First of all, it can bring new life to his self-image. A minister from Utah wrote, "The affirmation of others, especially in the church, really picked me up and helped me to see that failure in marriage was not failure as a person." And a minister from eastern Washington wrote, "As soon as it was clear that my church, family, and society/community were accepting/supporting of me in divorce, I thought better of myself."

In my own struggle with my self-image, I was ministered to in many ways by the affirmations of church people. Several people whom I didn't even know well made a point of coming up to me in the hospitality hour after morning worship to tell me that they were praying for me and that they felt I was doing a good job. This was very affirming, even though I knew that there were people who felt differently. Several boys in the high school group with which I worked came up to me privately to see how I was doing.

Even more importantly, people helped me to find a new view of myself. Before the divorce, I had tried to see myself as the "nice guy" who would never hurt anyone. Often I had to overlook my own selfishness to maintain the "Image," even to myself. But with the divorce, this had to change. I had to find a new perception of myself. I didn't want to be another convert to the "me" generation, but I knew I could no longer be the "nice guy" who never thinks of himself. Friends at the Topeka church, and from the Wamego church as well, helped me to understand that I could express my needs and my negative feelings and they would still see me as a caring person. They shared with me the love they saw in me, even though they also saw the selfishness, anger, and hurt. In that process they helped me find and affirm myself.

A second way emotional support is vital to a minister is in helping him to reaffirm his ministry. In looking at the responses of the ministers in my survey, I am convinced that the love and support of a congregation can often be the decisive factor in whether a minister leaves the ministry or goes on to a more dynamic work in the church. One minister who is now in a denominational position wrote, "The church stood with me, and this was the difference in my survival as a minister. I was informed that I had loved and cared for them in their time of need and that I need not run. They would care and support. It was redemptive behavior."

Gary Demarest, a divorced minister now serving a Presbyterian church in California, wrote of his experience after his divorce in his book *Christian Alternatives Within Marriage*:

It was my assumption that our failure in marriage called for the automatic termination of my pastoral career.

For the dear people of the Riverside Presbyterian Church in Jacksonville, Florida, who wouldn't let me run away from the reach of their love; for the fathers and brothers of the Presbytery of Suwannee who were firm but always kind; for the friends across the country who affirmed me in Christ's love when I couldn't love myself—I'll always be grateful. Had it not been for people in Jacksonville like Bill and Toddle Beaufort and Rex Dunlap I would not have known these past twenty years of joyous service as a clergyman and pastor.[3]

In an age when ministers are trying to encourage the ministry of the laity, such incidences show how real and important the laity's ministry to the clergy can be.

When a minister divorces, there is mourning by the minister, the minister's family, and the community of faith. Perhaps there is also conflict. But just as real as the mourning and conflict are the newfound love, support, and understanding that can grow out of the experience. When the "Image" falls and someone *is* there to pick up you, the imperfect human being, then love takes on new meaning. And in that new meaning, life comes where death had been.

I come
   to you
a child
      who has
      lost himself—
frightened
         confused
                  alone—
Looking
   not for a
parent
      gone astray
      but
      for
an image
   within myself
      to guide me.

I come
   to you
scared
      but drawn
   by
      your
         loving touch.

I come
   to you
scared
      but
         reaching out
      to
         a
            vision
         I find
      within
            you.

Be gentle
for I am discovering
myself
in you.

What About the Minister's Ex-Spouse?

A few years ago James Taylor sang a song called "Her Town Too." The song shares how, with divorce, there is also a sense of alienation from the community of which a person used to feel a part.

In the case of many former wives of ministers the idea could be rephrased to say, "It used to be her church, too." (While an effort will be made in this chapter to discuss the situations of both former husbands and former wives of ministers, the data about former husbands is limited.[1]) Although many divorced ministers get support, this is far less often the case with former spouses of ministers. If the minister is supported and stays with the church, the former spouse is often left abandoned. "It used to be her (his) church, too," but after the divorce he or she is often a spiritual orphan.

That former spouses often get little support is particularly significant when we understand how much pain the former spouse goes through. One former wife from Idaho wrote (in reference to the "fishbowl" existence of clergy marriage), "I felt as if the fishbowl was polluted and the fish were dead." And a woman from Illinois who was formerly married to a minister wrote, "I'd rather have been dead than divorced and considered how I might take my life in a way that appeared natural, so my children wouldn't be hurt more." While my sample of former wives was smaller than my sample of clergy, their responses were more uniformly full of such descriptions of pain than were the responses from the divorced clergy.

Some of the pain experienced by former spouses of clergy is that which is experienced in most divorce situations: loneliness and loss of intimacy. The previously mentioned woman from Idaho expressed this well when she said, ''I no longer had a special place in the heart of a man and I felt crippled without the lovemaking and companionship— the sharing of my life at the deepest level.'' There is also the pain that comes from disillusionment. A former spouse from western Washington shared, ''I had real difficulties pulling myself out of feeling as if I was 'nothing' without a man. I grew up in the Cinderella-complex age when a man was supposed to make you happy, care for you, make you complete, and so on. My former spouse nurtured that idea.'' And there is the pain that comes from the disruption of a whole community of family relationships. One former wife shared, ''My family's back East, and so my spouse's family was mine. That changed right away! I was on my own. . . .''

In addition to these stresses, however, there are other areas of pain that are aggravated by the fact that the person was married to a minister. Financial problems are one such area. Divorce always brings financial stress. But such stress is aggravated for the former spouse of a minister, especially if the couple lived in a parsonage. The parsonage is always for the minister, and so the spouse must move, with no equity in a house to take along. And to make matters worse, some parsonages are furnished: so the former spouse does not even end up with many furnishings to take along.

Adding to the financial difficulty is the trouble many former spouses have in getting a share of retirement benefits. One former minister's wife wrote:

> An area of difficulty for me arose when I realized that while the churches my husband served demanded a great deal of me and expected a ''team'' ministry—one which I easily and willingly embraced—M & M [the Ministers and Missionaries Benefit Board] doesn't look at it that way. In this state, that could not now happen with the new laws—spouses will most likely be reimbursed for their contribution to the other's career upward mobility, etc.

Women divorced from ministers in other denominations have similarly experienced loss of any right to such benefits.[2]

When I talked to a representative of the Ministers and Missionaries Benefit Board, he told me that the pension benefits, like salary, belong to the paid employee and that like other property, they were subject to division in a divorce settlement. He added that the M and M Board obviously has to work within court orders and the laws of each of the fifty states and that the whole area of pension rights is rapidly changing. He did offer that the Board allows former spouses to purchase medical coverage for two years after the divorce.

Another factor that aggravates financial stress is the difficulty of getting into the job market. In this area former husbands are probably not as much affected as former wives of ministers. While this problem is common to many divorced women, it is aggravated by the fact that many churches traditionally have expected a lot of involvement from the minister's wife which has, until recently, prevented many of them from pursuing their own careers. The woman from Idaho who responded to my questionnaire listed the difficulty of "getting back into the job market after thirteen years" as one of the challenges she had to face. A former wife from Washington was more emphatic in writing:

> For me, one of the greatest problems has been the length of the marriage and the fact that when I was married, the spouse was such an "expected" partner in the ministry. This meant that my career goals were always second place. While I have a successful career now, I will never regain the years that I spent supporting my husband's ministry rather than cultivating my own future. I, of course, made that choice and am not sorry. Many wives have no career, at least in my age group. I know of one minister's wife who is facing divorce this year after thirty-eight years of marriage; career choices for her are difficult.

As with the divorced minister, part of the pain of divorce for the minister's former wife is in struggling with her identity. As Patricia Coots has written, "Wherever she goes, there is that awesome moment when she realizes that her identity is no longer that of minister's wife."[3] Several ex-wives mentioned this identity question when writing to me. One woman from eastern Washington wrote, "I continually reminded myself that I was no longer a minister's wife and that all the benefits I had taken for granted for so long were no longer mine." And the former wife from Idaho wrote, "My identity (my profession?) as the minister's wife was gone." In the latter case at least, the role of minister's wife was desirable enough that when this woman remarried, she married another minister. In other cases, the women may not have enjoyed the role, but still found it hard to change identity.

For some former wives, this change in identity is aggravated because they see their role as their vocation. Bouma suggests that there are some women who are so taken with their role they could be called "professional minister's wives."[4] Perhaps they grew up at a time when women didn't become ministers, and so being a minister's wife was the closest they could come. Thus one minister's former wife wrote:

> When I married as a youth, we were both in Bible school and it was my intention as well as his to be in the full-time ministry of the Lord and the church. I felt it was fulfilled in the marriage until we separated—then I felt very cheated that at this time of my life, after all the experience and years of productivity that youth has on its side were over, I was suddenly no longer in that position. I had to change and search for another avenue of service.

Former wives of ministers also sometimes have to deal with some serious self-image problems. These problems are aggravated by the fact that spouses have often been co-conspirators in the ministers' being part of the "Image." The "Image" not only says that the pastor has to be a perfect example of all that is good and holy, but that the pastor's family must be the same. This aggravates the problems ex-spouses can have with guilt and loss of self-worth. That they have fallen short of the "Image" means that they have let God down. Thus a former wife who initiated her divorce action wrote, "I felt that I was no longer acceptable and that I had certainly let down the profession, God, and the church. Guilt was a giant." She went on to say that because of this guilt, "I didn't feel worthy of any support; so the small amount I got— from a few personal friends—was appreciated." Another former wife, now living in Kentucky, also expressed such feelings, writing, "I had to overcome a tremendous amount of guilt for divorcing a minister (partly because I was a 'preacher's kid' myself)."

Some self-image problems relate to being a divorced Christian, especially for one who had once been part of a ministerial family. Several women whose clergy spouses filed for divorce shared that they had to face being divorced Christians, even though they personally are opposed to divorce. The woman from Illinois wrote in my survey:

> People just couldn't understand how a minister could divorce his wife. And I felt totally unable to answer, because I couldn't understand it either— it just shouldn't be a part of a Christian's life—and more so a minister. Somehow it seemed less acceptable for a minister to be divorced than others, even though there really isn't a double standard. I still struggle with this—it makes me feel so disgraced and stigmatized. . . .

We can note here again how the "Image" plays a part in suffering. She didn't file for divorce. She didn't want it. She doesn't believe in it. But there is little one can do to stop it if this is what the other person wants. So she shouldn't feel guilty, but she does. She feels guilty because she and others had bought the "Image." They were supposed to be part of the ministerial family, which is above such things. And so she continues to struggle with the "Image" and ask, "What went wrong? This wasn't supposed to be!"

The former wife from Kentucky was more rebellious against the "Image," writing that the church could have been more supportive "by not looking on us as if we were on a pedestal—letting us be people as they are." She went on to say, "That's asking a lot—to get rid of that mystique. I think my then-husband and I maintained that image— I was taught it from childhood and he must have 'caught' it."

When people have such self-image problems, regaining a feeling of self-worth is often difficult in any divorce situation. But this task is especially hard for a minister's spouse who has been accustomed to being considered to be on an elevated plane. Regaining self-worth can even be a problem when the other person takes most of the blame. One former wife wrote, "He has told me that it is not me, but rather he, who has the problems, and he is probably right. But that doesn't take away the devastation of rejection and the feeling of being good only to be thrown away."

When divorce comes, some clergy spouses must deal not only with the guilt that comes from within but also with the fact that others seek to place the majority of the blame on them. This happens sometimes because, to a degree, the pastor is still protected by the "Image." If the pastor is still seen as an ideally holy and spiritual person, the divorce cannot be his (her) fault. So it must be the spouse's fault! This reaction was described by a minister's former wife from Washington, who wrote:

> There is a stigma attached to having been married to a minister. People react in shock and unbelief. I have tried to keep the fact quiet . . . yet the word gets around and I find it a source of pain. After all, it must be my fault the marriage didn't work, mustn't it?

One divorced minister who shared his experience with me told me that there was this kind of tendency in his congregation. While he received much support, she received little, and one lay person even went to his ex-wife to tell her that the divorce happened because she "needed to get right with the Lord."

It needs to be understood by all persons involved that ministers are perfectly capable of contributing their share to marital problems! In fact, when a minister doesn't think that he is contributing to such problems, he is probably contributing *more* than his share.

It should also be said, in light of the fact that even the minister's former spouse is affected by the "Image," that the person who divorces or is divorced by a minister is no less loved by God than any other person who is struggling and hurting. In a sense, the former spouses of ministers can find spiritual kinship with Hagar. Hagar was one of two mates of Abraham, who perhaps more than anyone else in Old Testament times was seen as "chosen of God." But Abraham "sent her away" because Sarah was jealous of Hagar and her son. It was probably particularly painful for Hagar to be rejected by one who was seen as "a man of God." Perhaps she felt that God would naturally be "on Abraham's side" and would also reject her. And with such feelings she probably also felt guilt and loss of self-worth, as we have noted that many former wives of ministers also experience. But God had a message for Hagar, which conveys a message for former spouses of ministers. God's encounter with Hagar is described in Genesis 21:14c-18. After she and her son had been sent away,

> . . . she departed, and wandered about in the wilderness of Beersheba. And the water in the skin was used up, and she left the boy under one of the bushes. Then she went and sat down opposite him, about a bowshot away, for she said, "Do not let me see the boy die." And she sat opposite him, and lifted up her voice and wept.
> And God heard the lad crying; and the angel of God called to Hagar from heaven, and said to her, "What is the matter with you, Hagar? Do not fear, for God has heard the voice of the lad where he is. Arise, lift up the lad, and hold him by the hand; for I will make a great nation of him."

Her son was chosen too! In that time and culture, this was essentially saying that *she* was also chosen. God had not rejected her just because Abraham had. And God gives the same message today. God does not take sides with the minister in clergy divorce. But rather God has chosen the former spouse as well—chosen her or him to receive God's love, healing, and service. The former wife from Illinois, who had once considered suicide, showed that she later had experienced the truth of this when she wrote:

> I know God has promised never to leave me, and he always loves me, and the people in my church and family, and his family, too, love me.

He's promised he has a good plan for me, and I believe it—nine days out of ten, anyway!

And yet, in spite of the fact that God does not abandon those who have been divorced from ministers, the same cannot be said of many churches. While the woman referred to above found love in her church, many former wives find only rejection. A former wife from eastern Washington wrote that "the church as a body did nothing to relieve my suffering—they were interested in helping my husband. . . ." She went on to say, "I felt that the church had taken sides and I was on the outside." Another former wife from Washington shared that "only one person [in the congregation] showed concern and love for me and she was already my friend." And an ex-spouse from Idaho wrote that for a long time she could not go back to her church because her ex-husband was still ministering there. When she finally did go back (she did not make clear if this was while her ex-husband was still there), she was told that she "made people uncomfortable." While it is understandable that people might be uncomfortable and while most former spouses do not want to go back to the church where their ex-husband is ministering, it would seem that, as the church, people should have concern for a hurt, suffering person instead of just for their own comfort.

The woman from western Washington who participated in my study related her feelings as the former wife of a minister about the insensitivity of the church to the needs of divorced people in general. She wrote, "I am much more aware of how terribly family-oriented everything is in the church—from potluck suppers to camping experiences. I still feel very much out of place in some of the settings."

Because of these experiences of lack of support, several of the women who corresponded with me have pulled away from the church. A woman who was divorced from her husband thirteen years ago wrote:

> During the first two years or so following, my family and I tried to become a part of another AB [American Baptist] church but in the end that didn't work. I have only rarely gone to church since and can't seem to escape the awful traumatic feelings that surface each time I go.

In another case a woman from Kentucky related her withdrawal from church both to her experience as the former wife of a minister and to her experience of having been a "preacher's kid." She wrote:

> I left the church. I was fed up with not being able to choose for myself. Since babyhood I'd "had" to go to church every Sunday—and after I was

married—play a role. I was genuine and felt comfortable at first, but eventually it wore thin.

She went on to say that she has recently started attending meetings of the Quakers, or the Religious Society of Friends.

In another case the spouse did not leave the church as such, but she did leave the denomination in which she had been when married.

Even in cases in which the ex-spouse remains active, there can be scars. One woman, formerly married to one minister and now married to another minister, nevertheless wrote, "Christian issues are harder for me to accept by faith. I don't quite trust the church anymore."

Certainly, not all of those who have been divorced from ministers feel rejected by the church. A former wife from Illinois notes that she felt accepted in both the church served at the time of the divorce and the one to which she moved shortly after the divorce. She wrote, "My commitment and involvement is greater than it has ever been." And a former wife of a minister in a denominational position shared that "many church members called, encouraged me, and did not pass judgment. I returned to the church and back to my position as church organist— not without difficulty, but with love and support." In my sample, five of the seven former wives of ministers felt little or no support and had their relationship to the church negatively affected. The other two felt support and are actively involved in their respective churches.

The degree to which those who had once been at the heart of church life as ministers' wives are feeling abandoned by the church is disturbing. Many feel that the church has turned its back on their pain and is not listening. When Patricia Evans Coots did a study of former ministers' wives for the United Methodist Church a few years ago, she found that many were eager to have someone show some concern about them. She noted that for many of these wives the questionnaire that she sent out was the first expression of concern they had received from anyone within the church.[5] And a questionnaire is not a very personal way of showing concern.

The church needs to start finding more ways of supporting those who get divorced from ministers. There is no reason why the church cannot show caring toward both minister and former spouse. In most cases the former spouse will not wish to stay in a congregation where her or his ex-spouse remains as minister, but the church can help the former spouse in whatever transitions need to be made. The pastoral relations committee, or whatever committee or board deals with such matters, should meet with the former spouse and determine together the ways the church can be helpful. If the family had been living in a parsonage, especially a furnished parsonage, a "starting over" shower could be appropriate.

Special care should be taken to help with the spiritual needs of the former spouse. If the person is staying in the community but feels the need to change churches, several people from the Sunday school class she attended could be designated as persons to accompany her in a church search. They could attend different churches with the former spouse until she finds one in which she is comfortable. They could even be useful in introducing the former spouse to people they know in those churches.

Until the former spouse finds a new church, it should be realized that she is a person without a minister. (In many respects most people who remain married to ministers are also persons without a minister! It's hard to be both spouse and minister to a person.) In the interim, lay people may need to designate someone or several people as unofficial ministers to the former spouse. Such a person or persons would take special care to keep in touch with the former spouse.

Denominational leaders also need to take a role in ministering to the former spouse. At present, such is not always done. In talking with several area ministers, district superintendents, and persons holding similar positions, I have found that nothing is generally done with a former spouse once the divorce is final. One former wife expressed her anger about this lack of support, saying that she felt deserted by her colleagues. The only contact that was made was "when the area minister felt compelled to see me to try to persuade me to reconcile." Such lack of support from the denomination prompted Patricia Evans Coots to write, ". . . the fact that the institution has no longer any responsibility for a woman who may have served many years with her husband is often painful. . . ."[6]

Denominational leaders need to take more responsibility for former spouses of ministers for two reasons. One is that, at least in the case of wives, the spouse has generally served the church in many ways for which she has not been paid. In many cases this service has been encouraged by both the church and denominational people. My own feeling is that too much is expected along this line, and that the minister's wife (or husband) needs to be given more room to be her (or his) own person. But the fact remains that people have had such expectations of the minister's spouse for a long time. And so, when the minister and spouse divorce, the denomination cannot say that they owe nothing to the former spouse in terms of support.

A second reason denominational leaders need to give such support is that the former spouse is a person without a minister. And if the former spouse moves out of the community, there is little the former congregation can do to fill the void. But denominational leaders can, through their contacts, make sure that someone from the denomination contacts the person in a new community.

Coots suggests two kinds of support that need to be given to former wives: support from other former wives of ministers and career-development counseling.[7] The denomination can and should help in both of these areas. It can help develop a network of former spouses who can be supportive of each other. It can and should work with other denominations in this task, as this is an area where denominational differences have little relevance. And the denomination should also help provide career-development counseling so the former spouse can start building for the future.

Finally, the denominations should, through their seminaries, do more preventive work by helping prepare future ministers' spouses for the pressure that will be put upon them. Some seminaries do this already. But there are many instances on record when this evidently has not been done. A Baptist minister from Utah wrote of his experience, "Seminary did little to help the soon-to-be pastors' wives deal with their fears regarding the expectations of the church, especially the women of the church." Other studies indicate that others have similarly been denied such preparation.[8]

While the needs and hurts of former spouses have been emphasized in this chapter, there are also positive things that happen to former wives. It has already been said that some experience support. It should also be said that the divorce can be a growing experience that results in personal benefits. The former wife from Illinois wrote:

> I have been forced to grow—I've learned to do a hundred things I never did before (many of which I hate, but still do!). But the good part is, I am free to serve the Lord, unhindered, and to love my children and grandchildren as I wish, not fearing my husband would feel bad or rejected
> . . . .

From Kentucky a former wife of a minister wrote regarding her experience, "I have felt free from many 'oughts'—some of them self-imposed I am sure. I feel free to grow and change and I am doing both."

Freedom was a benefit that was also mentioned by a former wife now living in New Mexico. She wrote:

> I did not seek our divorce in order to gain a sense of freedom, but that freedom is one of the greatest "goods"—freedom to think, to act, to bloom, to dance, to feel passionate, to meet all kinds of people, and freedom to become financially comfortable.

Other positive benefits mentioned by those divorced from ministers include: more time for one's own career, greater financial and personal independence, and the challenge and the opportunity to develop new skills.

So the picture is not entirely bleak. But the tragedy is that it could be much brighter if more former spouses of ministers could find love and support from the local church and denominational leadership.

We are not dealing here with an issue of the minister versus the former spouse. The issue is the pain of both persons versus the lack of concern or awareness of the church and general public. *Both* partners can and should find support from the Body of Christ. Are we not called to "bear one another's burdens"? How much more are we called to do so with persons who have spent much of their lives seeking to bear the burdens of others! It is hoped that this chapter will help us better fulfill that mission.

Life as a Divorced Minister

The best way to learn about life is not through books, but through living. And to learn about the pains and struggles of life, one must live them. This is exactly what the divorced minister has done. Of course, the minister did not get divorced in order to learn about the pains of life, and most, if given the opportunity, would have opted for another "course of study." Nevertheless, nearly all of those who responded to my questionnaire experienced their divorce as a time of profound growth and learning. It is learning that no seminary can offer.

Because the life experience of the divorced minister is an experience of learning, it is important that that life experience be shared with those groups of people who most need to learn what the divorced minister goes through. These include parishoners and denominational leaders who want to be supportive, friends and family members who want to understand what is happening, and those clergy and spouses who are considering divorce themselves.

The first thing that needs to be understood about what life is like for the divorced minister is that it starts with pain. This cannot be over-emphasized. Perhaps the best description I have heard was that of a divorced woman who said, "Divorce is emotionally like a massive heart attack that leaves you disabled and in pain."[1] Most of all the ministers I corresponded with reported such pain. A Baptist minister from New Hampshire was typical in writing, "I experienced divorce as the most negative experience I have ever had. I felt negated as a person."

A person who expects divorce to be other than painful is in for a rude awakening. Those who call divorce "an easy out" do not know what they are talking about. There is nothing easy about it. The divorced minister knows this and hence can help others understand why it is important to try everything possible to keep a marriage alive before one decides for divorce. Thus, one respondent from Washington, D.C., wrote that, when he counsels people considering divorce, he "tells the persons of the pain involved" and asks them if they really think it is worth the pain.

The pain is there for the divorced minister, regardless of whether or not he or she was the one who initiated legal action. Of those responding to my questionnaire, twenty-four of thirty-nine filed for divorce in their divorce action. In four other situations both parties filed. But virtually all of them talked of how much the divorce hurt. As John Landgraf has written, "The pain of the rejector may be of a different sort than that of the rejected one, but divorce always results in pain for both parties and that pain can be enormous and pervasive."[2]

The pain of the one who initiates the divorce comes in large part from guilt at being the one to make the decision to end the marriage. Thus one New Jersey minister who filed her divorce action wrote, "I feel a lot of guilt at not being able to work out some kind of reconciliation. I get defensive and find that I refuse to talk about the situation with most people."

The initiator also has to act in a context of a painful awareness that there was at least some good in the marriage that is being left behind. It's like having to amputate your own diseased leg. You know it has to be done, but the hurt can be tremendous.

The pain of the one who did not make the decision is in the tremendous feeling of rejection and the loss of self-worth that accompanies such rejection. A Southern Baptist minister, whose ex-spouse filed, shared that the divorce "took my self-worth and fragmented it into a million pieces. My self-image, for the first time in my life, was devastated." Such persons see a vital part of their lives being taken away and very little that they can do about it. Sometimes they do not even understand why the divorce happened. And this uncertainty makes it hurt all the more.

Both parties experience pain from other sources as well. There is the pain of failure. A number of ministers referred to this as a source of pain in their own situations. A minister from New York wrote, "Divorce hurts. There is most certainly an element of failure; you fail yourself, your children, your wife, your calling. . . ." And a minister from Massachusetts wrote:

> I was aware of my own failure; I was guilt-stricken. After such a long marriage and having my identity formulated through that relationship as wife and mother, I was to a certain extent "imageless." I feel that I am just now (after three years of separation and one year of divorce) really moving out and away from the failure and guilt of that marriage.

There is also the pain that comes from memories. Even a marriage that is basically destructive has good times. I know that there were good times in my previous marriage. And even though I am happier now, I feel pain when I remember those good times. Divorce is a *loss*. One loses part of one's life, the good with the bad. I have come to realize that until I have dealt with what happened as a loss (however beneficial the change was overall) I have not really dealt with the experience at all. And while I have made much progress, I still have some mourning of this loss to do.

How long it takes to recover from the pain of the loss of divorce can vary from person to person. Some of it depends on whether partners are in agreement with the decision to divorce. In my case, I decided to file for divorce. The pain of my situation was at its most intense level during the period of six to eight months or so before I filed. It was then that I really wrestled with what to do. From the time I filed, my pain started to abate and that of my former wife, who was not in agreement with the divorce, began to intensify.

In general, ministers in my survey seemed to be hurting to some degree for at least a couple of years after the divorce. A minister from Kentucky shared that "for a time the quality [of my life] was drastically affected (one to two years), but now I am happy being single with a good support system of both singles and marrieds." And a minister serving in a denominational position in California told how for her it took "several years of therapy to rediscover self and learn I was OK."

For others, however, the process takes longer, and some fear they will never recover. A minister from Wisconsin shared that "it has taken five years to resolve most of the emotional loss, but I doubt if it will ever be completely resolved." And a minister from Connecticut shared that she felt she would always have regrets, even though her former husband was an atheist opposed to her work and later revealed himself to be a homosexual. She wrote, "He is still faithful to the children, reliable with his obligations to me and still basically a fine man. I still mourn him and our loss, but I know in the long run I am more content. But I will probably go to my grave with regrets."

Most see growth coming out of their pain. A minister from Washington, D.C., was typical in writing, "I went from the pits of hell—I considered suicide because I was a failure (it seemed) in all areas—to extreme confidence and strength of having gone through one of life's most difficult problems and growing from it." And a minister from New York, who had also been widowed in one of her marriages, wrote that "I prefer to see all the troubles I have had in life as discipline and opportunities for growth." She went on to say that although painful things remain, they "diminish in time and as positive things keep happening."

God's presence is a very important element in this growth. The divorced minister learns experientially that God is not a God who is there just when she is preaching to a packed church or when grateful people are singing praises for a program well-planned. God is a God who is there at the most painful moments of life, even painful moments to which one's own sin has contributed. God is a God whose very nature is to heal and to redeem. And when the divorced minister has experienced the healing of his or her own pain, then redemption has become more than a word.

As a whole, the ministers who corresponded with me felt their lives were, *in time*, improved by the divorce. A minister serving a chaplaincy in Kansas wrote, "It has improved the quality of my life because now I feel free to be myself. For many years I had to live a 'lie' of pretending that I was the happy, ideal, pastoral figure." A minister from Utah wrote, "I enjoy life very much with the cloud of impending disaster no longer overhead." And a minister now serving in a denominational position in Washington State shared "I believe that having worked through the divorce, the loss, and the failure, I am a stronger and more whole person."

The positive effects of divorce on a person's life come from various factors. One factor mentioned by several ministers was a new sense of self-respect. A minister from Washington State wrote, "I respect myself for making this most important decision . . . and for having the guts to do it . . . for me!'' And a chaplain from Kansas shared, "I grew to the place where I could tell the world that I was a capable person who would not live in hell while pretending to be holy.'' Several ministers wrote that self-images which had been devastated in bad marriages were revived and made healthy again after divorce.

The factor of self-respect is certainly a vital one. The one person you *have* to live with is yourself. If because of a bad marriage you are feeling bad about yourself over a long period of time, it is bad for both your own health and your relationship to others in the world. It is bad for your health because a bad self-image leads to depression, which sooner or later starts to destroy your body. It is bad for your relationship to others because when you don't feel good about yourself, you have little to give to others. In the ministry that is devastating to your calling. If you can rescue yourself from such a situation by saving the marriage, that is the way to go. But if such cannot be done, you have to act to keep your spirit from dying altogether. Your self-respect and sense of worth are your spiritual breath of life. You can only hold your breath for so long before fighting to get breath however you can get it.

Another positive effect several ministers cited as coming from their divorce was the release from hostilities. A minister serving a chaplaincy in Illinois wrote, "For many years the power struggle and fighting were the central facts of life for me. . . . Being free of that power struggle and fighting for my own sense of integrity has given me a new sense of freedom and power.'' Another minister cited the "peaceful home environment, lack of tension and unspoken hostilities'' as a positive aspect of her new life situation.

The effect of hostilities in a marriage intensifies over a period of time. As it developed in my own situation my attitude went from one of hope of remedying the basic problems to one of despair of ever taking care of the root issues. It was then that these hostilities began to make me feel constantly ill at ease in my own home. When I moved out during our initial separation, I felt immediate relief at being able to have a home where I was free from this tension. True, it was just a small apartment with a few pieces of old or rented furniture. But it was a place where I could withdraw from tensions instead of increasing them. And for me that is an important quality for a home to have.

Certainly there are times when there is tension in any home shared by more than one person. Such tension is necessary for a family to grow and make adjustments to one another. But when such tension is constant and does *not* result in the necessary growth, it becomes oppressive. Then the tension blocks being able to have a home where one can feel "at home."

For some ministers, divorce also brought new opportunities for friendships. A minister from New York wrote, "I was tired of not doing things, going places, enjoying life, socializing with people. I now have more friendships than ever before." And a minister from Massachusetts shared, "My life has been enhanced greatly by my divorce because it has lead to many more friendships . . . than were possible prior to my divorce."

Other positive benefits from divorce which were listed by ministers included: improvement in health, opportunity to pursue educational goals, and greater independence.

Even though most ministers felt that the quality of their lives was eventually improved by their divorces, they acknowledged that there are negative effects even beyond the initial pain one encounters. The most common of these are loneliness and difficulties relating to children of the marriage.

Loneliness is a common problem for divorced ministers who remain single. A Methodist minister who remains single wrote, "I do not enjoy living alone, and find loneliness to be the most detrimental aspect of my lifestyle." An Episcopal minister shared that for him life as a divorced person is a "mixed bag." He went on to write, "I like the independence and the greater sense of being myself—and then there is the loneliness (or an opportunity to learn more of myself in that loneliness)." Another Methodist minister, who is now married, referred to his years of singlehood as "six years of loneliness." He added that "while divorced, I was lonely, hurting, anxious, and sometimes quite depressed."

Part of the reason why loneliness is a problem is that dating and socializing can be difficult for ministers. Ministers have busy work schedules and have limited time, and many people are hesitant to date ministers or even to ask them to social gatherings. They are afraid that if a minister is around they must "watch how they act." Complicating these difficulties is the fact that many ministers have churches in small communities where there are few social opportunities.

With such problems in socializing, some ministers turn even more to their work. Thus a minister from New Jersey wrote, "I've become a workaholic since I don't have much else to do, and my social life is the pits."

Other ministers turn rather quickly to marriage to remedy loneliness. But John Landgraf, a counselor from the Center for the Ministry in Oakland, California, who has been divorced himself, warns against this approach. He writes, "In my practice nowadays I am seeing many Protestant ministers who are single, most often by divorce, and I am concerned about their apparent eagerness to remarry as soon as possible."[3] He believes one must do much emotional growing and must really experience who one is as a single before going on to remarriage.

I find myself in the rather awkward position of agreeing with Landgraf while not having followed that advice myself. I remarried five months after my divorce was finalized. I do not in the least bit regret that decision because my marriage has worked out extremely well to this point. However, marrying soon after a divorce does entail risk. Loneliness can prompt a peson to marry out of the intensity of need instead of out of a more positive vision of what the two persons have to give to each other and how their personalities match. Emotionally, it is much better to deal as completely as possible with the endings of one life situation before going on to the beginnings of a new life situation. This is pointed out well in William Bridges' book *Transitions*.[4]

I can only say in defense of my own decision that I took the risk with several factors in mind. I was actually alone for ten months previous to my remarriage, as my former wife and I separated a month-and-a-half before I filed and the divorce took four months to finalize. During that time I was in group counseling, which helped me to learn about myself and deal with my own anger and sense of loss. Counseling also helped me to think through what I had contributed to the problems of the previous marriage (some of this had also come out in the marriage counseling I had had with my former wife). I do not believe that I decided to remarry out of loneliness, as I was really far lonelier in the last year or so of my marriage than I was while I was single. Nor do I believe I decided out of a need to be married, as I had looked forward at the time of filing to being free from *any* marriage obligations for some time. I was then, and still am, convinced that I decided to remarry because in Cathy I found the qualities that I had always wanted in a wife. Since I was facing a probable move to another area of the country,

I decided I would rather take the risks involved in early remarriage than risk leaving behind one who had so many of the qualities for which I had been looking.

While I took the risk of an early remarriage, I still would assert that it *is* a risk. In general a far better approach is to have a transitional time of at least a year or two before remarrying.

Another reason why remarriage is not necessarily the most appropriate cure for loneliness is that in time one can learn to conquer loneliness as a single. One Methodist minister who has been single for six years wrote that his loneliness is "minimal compared to at first." He went on to say, "I have worked on loneliness being OK." What loneliness remains can be OK because it gives one an opportunity to learn about one's self, an Episcopal minister noted. It does not have to ruin one's life. A campus minister shared, "Though I have experienced loneliness, I have developed many new friends, had several good love relationships, and have developed new personal skills and interests."

Learning to conquer loneliness is an important life learning experience for a minister, who must deal frequently with lonely people. If he or she has conquered loneliness in his or her own life, then it is easier to share from the heart with others who face similar circumstances.

Another area in which there are lingering negative effects is in relation to children. Parents who have custody or primary residence have the stress of raising children alone. This is particularly difficult for a minister who has irregular hours and may have to find childcare on the spur of the moment because of an emergency in the church family. Even with older children there is the need for someone to help with disciplining and role modeling. One minister from Connecticut shared that she had this need with her thirteen-year-old son, and that one of the couples of the church had stepped in to show him extra attention.

Those who do not have their children living with them have the problem of missing the children. A change in positions is likely to take such a minister away from the town, and even the state, where his or her children remain. Several ministers shared that missing their children was a problem. A chaplain from Tennessee shared, "I miss children in my daily life." A minister from Oregon wrote, "What I miss the most is my role as parent. I miss the family." And a minister from Utah confided that "children who reside out of state" were primary concerns.

Being away from my children is the most serious negative aspect of my life as a divorced minister. I have two daughters, Angie, who is eleven, and Carina, who is seven. I have been close to Angie from the time of her birth. She was born while I was in seminary. I remember when as an infant she had colic and woke up three or four times a night crying. I took my turn getting up and rocking her back to sleep in a rocking chair, while singing her songs that were so off-key that no adult would have tolerated it! As Angie grew older, I always enjoyed putting her to bed and either singing a song or reading a story to her. This was always important to her. In recent years we enjoyed going out regularly for special time together, to play video games or to bowl. Sometimes the only time we could find was from nine to eleven at night. This wasn't the best thing on school nights, I know, but they were precious times.

Although Angie is shy, she shares her feelings with me rather well, even during sad times, like the time when the divorce occurred. I can still remember her tears when I left for my apartment the first time.

We adopted Carina when she was three. Carina is as out-going as Angie is shy. She is a child who can dominate the attention of a group when she enters a room. She loves to be hugged and cuddled, and she is capable of great empathy for those who are hurting. She makes friends fairly easily with other children, but she does have some behavioral problems that derive from being neglected by her natural mother. She has a hard time feeling accepted and loved, and sometimes feels she must fight with her older sister for equal privileges. But inside, she is an injured little girl who is as eager to give love as to receive it. She also enjoys my stories and my songs. I used to like to take her swinging in the park.

The divorce was hard on Carina, too. She had already gone through a great deal, and she couldn't express her feelings well. She frequently asked, "If you and Mommy get a divorce, you will still be my daddy, won't you?" I would respond "Yes," but it is impossible to give a five-year-old as much reassurance as she needs at such a time.

Now I live over seventeen hundred miles from my children. They have adjusted fairly well to the divorce. But I only get to see them for six weeks or so in the summer and during Christmas or Thanksgiving. For the rest of the year, I experience the hurt of being away from them.

A song at night
        to bring your sleep
A gentle hug
        whenever you'd weep
These I loved to give
        when together we did live.

But many miles are between us now
        and the love I want to show somehow
    must come in other ways—
        a card
            a note
                a letter I wrote
        a phone call to help cross the miles
            a prayer to touch your heart again
                    when I cannot touch your hand.

These are not the same
                I know
    But they are all I have to show
            I love you as before
And no matter what else comes our way
        the love I have is going to stay
        and all I have within my heart
                    is yours
                while we're apart.

And the songs I sang not long ago
        I'll sing out all the more
When with tears of love
            I hold you close
        as I often did before.

We write frequently and I try to call every month, but I have missed a lot of bedtimes.

In this chapter I have sought to share the life experiences of divorced ministers. They are experiences from which all can learn, although such learnings cannot always be categorized and summarized into neat little truths. But suffice it to say that the divorced minister has lived through a very painful experience in life. And in that living, she or he has grown.

Ministering After the Fall

L ife goes on after divorce. But does ministry? The initial reactions many ministers encounter, both from others and from themselves, are negative. "No preacher can be divorced and still serve the Lord" was the attitude one Presbyterian minister said he encountered in his congregation. And having encountered that attitude myself, I know he is not alone in his experience. For other ministers, the doubt comes from within themselves. Several who wrote to me said that they initially assumed their ministry was over.

But ministry need not end when one is divorced. In fact, this can be just the beginning. The key issues relating to the effect of divorce on ministry are how receptive the church and the denomination are to the divorced minister and how the divorce affects the person's ability to minister.

Divorce does affect the receptivity of some churches and denominational leaders to a person's ministry, but perhaps not as much as some might think. When ministers were asked on my questionnaire, "Did your divorce affect your retaining your church position or getting a new one?" twenty of the thirty-seven who responded to the question said, "No." Only fifteen said it had an effect, and two others were uncertain. Of course, it must be understood that those who responded were solicited through denominational channels and did not include anyone who had permanently left the ministry. There are ministers who have left the ministry permanently after a divorce, possibly because opportunities were denied them. My survey does not really reflect the experience of these people. Nevertheless, the fact that the majority of even those still in ministry could say that their opportunities to minister have not been limited by their divorce, is better than many would expect. One minister from California has even gone through two divorces while retaining his same church position, and a Presbyterian executive told me of a Presbyterian minister who had done the same.

Such openness to the ministry of a divorced person comes in spite of (or perhaps *because* of) the tendency of most divorced ministers to be quite frank about the divorce. One minister from New Jersey wrote:

> The pulpit committee of my new position said that whether or not I was divorced was my business and none of theirs and that if they were hiring in any other business, they wouldn't even ask. They didn't ask, but I wouldn't accept their invitation to candidate unless they knew that I was coming alone and intended to file for divorce when the necessary time limit for separation ran out. They went back and discussed it and called me back with their invitation unchanged.

This kind of receptivity can also sometimes come in spite of the minister's own expectations and anxieties. An Episcopal minister wrote:

> I wondered how the congregation and my bishop and rector would see this. I wondered if I would be seen in a bad light or as a failure and if my chances of moving to another congregation would be hindered. None of these worries, however, proved to be valid.

If the marital problems were serious enough, divorce could even help the prospects of a minister. A bad marriage can be so disruptive to ministry that divorce becomes necessary in order for one to minister at all. A minister from Washington State shared that he lost a number of opportunities because of the effect his marriage had on his ministry. He is now out of the ministry but plans to reenter soon. A Methodist minister shared, "I was told that resolution of the marriage situation was a prerequisite for me to conclude my leave-of-absence status and be appointed to a church. Hence, I decided to file."

In other cases, continued marital problems have already forced a change in type of ministry by the time of the divorce. A minister in a hospital chaplaincy in Illinois wrote:

> There was a cause-effect relationship between our conflicts and church problems that none of us were able to manage very creatively. In the end, my moving into hospital ministry was, in part, a way to escape this whole problem.

Thus, divorce does not always mean that the minister will have greater

71240

difficulty getting a new position. Sometimes it has no effect, and sometimes it may even improve prospects. However, in at least some instances, divorce makes it harder for a minister to find an opportunity to use his or her gifts in ministry to the degree that would otherwise be possible. Sometimes this means taking a smaller church with less pay. Sometimes it even means leaving the ministry for a while. Several ministers mentioned having gone that route.

In my own case I had to sell beef-jerky displays to grocery stores for a little over a month because I couldn't find a position, in part because of my divorce. Having to take such secular work does have benefits. I was able to get in touch once again with what it's like for lay persons in their jobs. It was even affirming to learn that I could do this kind of work. Other ministers mentioned similar benefits from having to take secular work for a period of time. But my calling and my identity are in the ministry, and I felt very much out of place when not in a ministerial position. I felt angry that I was not able to find opportunities to minister in the way I knew I could. I felt angry because I knew that the divorce was a factor in some cases. I was feeling like "defective merchandise" even though I knew I was quite capable. I was able to work through these feelings, largely because of the support and affirmation of others. But for ministers who do not get such support and affirmation, I am sure the process is much harder.

If a minister is divorced a second time, it most always means loss of ministerial opportunities. There are exceptions, as I have mentioned. But in three of the four cases in which ministers reported second divorces to me, the second divorce severely restricted their ministerial opportunities. A campus minister from Oregon who has been in the ministry for twenty-nine years wrote, "I definitely lost my standing in terms of moving to larger churches. After the second divorce I have been reduced to entry positions."

In the case of women ministers who divorce, the process of finding new positions is complicated by the fact of being female. It's always a little hard to know why one is rejected for a position. But when a woman minister is divorced, there are two factors that some churches may hold against her, and it's not always clear which one is creating the greatest difficulty. A minister from Massachusetts wrote, "Some churches would not interview me because I am female—or female and divorced." She went on to say that she was nevertheless able to secure a position without much trouble, but others are not so fortunate. A minister from New York told how the factors of her divorce and her gender combined in her situation:

> I was refused the pulpit in my home church; they sent me a letter stating the Bible says ministers should be the husband of one wife. So as a divorced and remarried [person] I was no longer qualified. The more powerful reason was that women are being [denied] local church leadership . . . [and a chance] to continue in the position of leadership *from the pulpit* and *over* men in the congregation. Excluding me from the pulpit as a remarried [person] sidestepped the reality that I was already ordained and female.

To a degree, the opportunities a minister has after a divorce may depend on what denomination the minister is in. The Southern Baptists who corresponded with me seem to have had the hardest time. A Southern Baptist serving in a chaplaincy wrote:

> My denomination has been very critical and judgmental of me. The leader of our State Convention told me that he considered me as a layman-nonprofessional—and had nothing that I could do for the Convention. Twice in a conversation he referred to me as a "persona non grata." American Baptists and other major denominations have welcomed and encouraged me. Southern Baptists have not.

Another Southern Baptist minister made a similar report saying, "My old hometown church has *not* been supportive, i.e., would not ordain me or give opportunity to preach there." A minister now serving an American Baptist church wrote that, at the time of the divorce, "I was affiliated with the Southern Baptist Convention. Few churches would look at me seriously. Hence, I figured on an institutional ministry and then joined the American Baptist Churches."

The reports of these ministers is consistent with what I was told by an area Director of Missions of the Southern Baptist Convention in Washington State, who generally does not recommend divorced ministers to churches. However, it needs to be understood that Southern Baptist churches operate independently, and that this attitude could vary from church to church and region to region. When I contacted the Southern Baptist Home Mission Board in Atlanta, I was told that it has no statistical information on the receptivity of churches to divorced ministers.

The approach of some denominations to the divorced minister tends to be positive. One Methodist district administrator, who himself has been divorced, told me that Methodist policy is to move a pastor after a divorce or give him or her a leave of absence. When such a minister is moved, every effort is made to make the move a "lateral" one, but that is not always possible when openings are limited. This policy is based on the belief that leaving a pastor in a church could cause factional disruption. However, the administrator to whom I spoke acknowledged that in his own situation he was *not* moved from the church where he was ministering at the time and the church was quite supportive of him.

The same administrator told me that while Methodists as a denomination are getting more lenient in matters of clergy divorce in general, they are getting stricter when adultery by the minister is involved. Previously, in cases of adultery, the ministers involved could often stay in the ministry, although they may have been forced to receive counseling and/or take a leave of absence. Now, the denomination is moving towards forcing those who have been involved in adultery to leave the ministry. In fact, in May 1984 the United Methodist governing conference adopted an explicit requirement for clergy of "fidelity in marriage and celibacy in singleness."

The effects of this new policy of the Methodists are, of course, yet to be seen. At best, the policy could help curb what is, as we mentioned in chapter 4, a serious problem. It could encourage ministers to look to more positive ways to find healing in their marriages or to resolve those problems by divorce, rather than getting involved sexually with someone else while still married. But at worst, it could merely force out of the church ministers for whom redemption as ministers is still possible. The policy could also be difficult to apply since it is not always clear when adultery has been involved. In such a situation rumor could be taken for truth. In the view of Paul Lowder, a problem already exists when denominational administrators respond to divorce and adultery involving clergy. He wrote in a 1979 issue of *The Circuit Rider*, "There is a difference between divorce and adultery, yet they seem to be dealt with identically."[1]

In my sample of Methodists, most of those who mentioned the attitude of their denominational leaders felt support, although one person did not. It is hard to tell whether adultery or suspicion of adultery was a factor in that particular case.

American Baptists have such a great deal of independence that how a divorced minister is received by a church probably varies from place to place. But none of the American Baptist ministers who wrote to me reported anything but support from their denomination. In my own case, both my area minister in Kansas and my area minister in Washington (who has also been divorced) have been quite helpful. Denominational staff in Kansas frequently expressed their desire to help me find a position in Kansas so I could remain in the region.

When I wrote to regional executives in my search for a new position, they were also helpful. However, most of them warned me that a divorced minister might have a hard time finding a position in their region, especially if one sought the position of senior pastor.

Research on the response of bishops in the Episcopal church has indicated that while a full range of responses can be found, bishops are most frequently positive and supportive toward divorced clergy.[2] While I only had responses from two Episcopal clergy in my survey, both reported receiving support from their denomination.

From the information I have been able to gather, it does seem that many mainline denominations are seeking to be supportive of their divorced clergy.

The one issue all denominations need to face is the issue of how to respond to sexual wrongdoing that results in divorce. I would not want to say that all divorced clergy should be encouraged to stay in the ministry, no matter what. Certainly, if a minister models lack of respect for marriage by getting involved in repeated extramarital affairs, the church can only be hurt by retaining such a person in the ministry. How to uphold ministerial standards and yet allow ministers to be humans who sometimes need redemption themselves is certainly a challenge. But a balance must be struck.

While receptivity of churches and denominations to the ministry of a divorced person varies, the view that divorced ministers have of their *ability* to minister is rather consistent. Nearly all of the ministers in my survey felt that they were *better* ministers for having gone through the experience of divorce. A minister from western Washington State wrote, "There is *no doubt* I am more effective as a minister and a human being since my divorce." A minister serving in a denominational position in California shared that "after our divorce I blossomed personally and professionally." And a minister from Colorado asserts that since her divorce she is a better minister and people "recognize the understanding" that has grown out of her experience.

A couple of ministers wanted to make clear that such improvement should not be taken as an encouragement for ministers to divorce. An Episcopal minister wrote, "I don't advise divorce as a way to enhance one's ministry—however when used as a time for learning and healing, it enhanced mine." And an American Baptist minister noted that "we certainly wouldn't encourage someone to experience something terrible in order to be a better minister, but it is a fact that going through troubled water does make you a better person and minister." Even Mary LaGrand Bouma, who does not see divorce as a legitimate option for any Christian, writes of divorced ministers, in *Divorce in the Parsonage*, "Often their ministry does not appear to be impaired. Although in some ways it is a detriment, in other ways, particularly in certain counseling situations, the experience can be a plus factor."[3]

Only one of the ministers who corresponded with me mentioned any negative effect divorce had on his ability to minister. This man wrote, "My professional life is probably at its lowest ebb. I don't seem to have the drive I did before. It may be due to being told by my ex-wife that my job was too important." But even this minister mentioned benefits to his ministry from the divorce. He wrote, "I am more compassionate, patient, slow to anger, rational, and willing to go the second mile with those whose lives are 'shot to hell.'"

The beneficial effects of divorce on one's ministry can come in several ways. They can come as a result of a person being released from a relationship which was detrimental to one's ministry. I have previously mentioned the minister from Connecticut who had been married to an atheist. She wrote, "I returned to school in 1979 against my husband's wishes. We held long conversations, but he was adamant that a divinity school education was 'crap.'" She went on to say that when she was in divinity school, her former husband "refused to give me one dime, much less any emotional support. It was very difficult." Fairly soon after she accepted her first church, he moved out.

Another minister from Massachusetts wrote that a personality trait of her husband held her back. She shared that "because of my former husband's possessiveness I knew it would be impossible for me to minister while married to him."

A bad marriage also ties up a lot of emotional energy, which is then released after a divorce. An Episcopal minister shared that since her divorce, "there is a sense of energy that was not there before." And a Methodist minister wrote in regard to his divorce that "it released me from a lot of negative energy and frustration."

In my own case, I found that with the increased energy also came a greater amount of creativity. Several people who worked with me in youth ministry commented that I seemed to show a greater amount of creativity in the programs that I planned and the curricula that I wrote after I filed for divorce. But even before they told me, I noticed this in myself. It is hard to be creative when one is full of unresolved tension, and that is how I had been previous to the divorce.

Ministry is also improved by the minister experiencing pain in life; this helps the minister understand the hurts of others. A minister from Utah wrote, "They [the congregation] see me as one who has been through it with them." A minister from Washington, D.C., reported that his divorce helped him to be a better minister by helping him understand the pain in himself and others. And a minister from Wisconsin shared, "When I have shared some of my own pain with others, it has opened many doors for good counseling and preaching."

People have a hard time having confidence that someone can help them if they don't feel that person understands their pain. One can't have much confidence in a "cure" that comes from a person who really doesn't understand why one is hurting in the first place. The divorced minister has experienced one of life's worst pains and from that experience can better help others with their pain.

The ability of the divorced minister to understand pain is particularly helpful in his or her work with other divorced people, and even in marriage counseling. Several ministers mentioned having a meaningful ministry with singles. A minister from Oregon was typical in writing:

> The number of divorced persons in our society is now about 50 percent. Many have remarried but that common experience has helped me to understand what they've been through. I have also had a significant ministry among single adults, 95 percent of whom are divorced.

Marriage counseling is enhanced in several ways. One is that the person or couple has a feeling that a divorced minister knows what their pain is like. This produces a trust that is helpful in the counseling process. A minister now serving in a denominational position in Washington State wrote, "There is a feeling of trust in marriage counseling because they believe you know something of their dilemma. . . ." A minister from New Jersey shared that, because of this trust, when she took a new church, a woman who was having marital problems confided in her immediately.

When I was divorced, one man came to me fairly soon afterwards to talk about his own possible divorce and the reaction of his son to the trauma of the situation. He came to me in large part because he knew I was going through the same thing. Eventually he decided to get back together with his wife, and I rejoiced with him in that decision.

In my time in Oakesdale, although the community is small, persons who have been facing divorce themselves or who are facing it in their family have been quite open in coming to me to talk. I'm sure that part of the reason they came so freely is that they know I understand what it is like and I won't be judgmental.

Another reason why divorce can help a minister in marriage counseling is that a divorced minister can often recognize problems in other marriages that occurred in his or her own marriage. A minister from Wisconsin asserted, "I am . . . much more aware of the danger signals others give off during marital struggles." This awareness helps the minister to assist the couple in confronting problems they may be trying to ignore.

If the minister has gone through marriage counseling prior to the divorce, this can also be a help in his or her own marriage counseling. A person who has gone through marriage counseling knows what the counselor did that was helpful and what was not helpful. It is also good for a counselor to know what it's like to be on the receiving end of such marriage counseling. It's hard to "swallow your pride" and go for marriage counseling, and sometimes it's hard to admit some of the things you have to admit in counseling. A counselor who knows this experientially can help a person feel more at ease.

Some people may think that a minister who has been divorced may be too ready to encourage other couples to divorce. But this does not seem to be the case with those who responded to my survey. On my questionnaire I asked, "In your marital counseling do you: (a) advise couples that divorce is *always* inappropriate; (b) advise couples that divorce is appropriate only after every effort has been made to reconcile, including marriage counseling; (c) advise couples that if they are unhappy, they should get divorced; (d) avoid counseling couples one way or another on whether or not they should get divorced; or (e) other." Of the thirty-eight persons who responded to this question, twenty-six answered "b," seven answered "d," and five answered "e." Responses under "e" included encouraging the persons to make their own decisions, helping the persons solve differences by loving Christ and each other, and sharing the minister's own experience and pain. No minister advised the couple to divorce simply because they were unhappy. Neither did any of the ministers advise that divorce is always wrong.

Divorced ministers do not encourage divorce readily simply because they know by experience that it is painful. Ministers who might too easily advise divorce would more likely be those who remain in unhappy marriages themselves. Such persons may look at divorce unrealistically, not knowing the pain involved.

Another reason why divorce can help a person be a better minister is that it can force the minister to depend on God for strength to a far greater degree. I know that before my divorce I had an increased sense of my own self-sufficiency. While in some areas I doubted my self-worth, I had a great deal of confidence in my own capability. I had confidence that I could handle everything I needed to handle. It wasn't that I left God out. I prayed for God's help and guidance. But I did not have the sense of utter dependence on God's strength that I had during my divorce. During that time everything became so overwhelming that I knew I could never handle it all without God's help. I came to identify very much with Abraham as he left the security of his past and went into the frightening unknown that the Promised Land must have been for him. My whole future was up for grabs, and nothing was certain. I learned from experience that the only way to face such a situation was to trust God. I did, and God came through for me. Having experienced in such a real way the truth of God's faithfulness and strengthening power, I can now proclaim it with all the more conviction to others.

Other ministers also shared that divorce deepened and strengthened their spiritual resources.

People need to believe in their own ability, and I certainly would not say that ministers should not do so. But when a person believes he can make it through life on his own strength alone, he is living with an illusion. Often one hesitates to take chances and avoids situations that might exceed one's ability and so shatter the illusion. Also, there is a certain amount of luck needed in avoiding overwhelming tragedy. Min-

In
   my
      Fall
   I tumbled
         long and far
      and wondered
               when it would end
         and
            if I would be
                     crushed
                  when I finally
               came to
            rest.

In
   my
      Fall
   I feared
         the unfocused swirling
      and
         empty spaces
      where I needed
            something
         to grab hold of.

In
   my
      Fall
   I found
         His hand
      and all that was
               crushed
            was an outer shell
         from which
            a new me
         emerged
            with wings.

Funny
   I never knew
that shell
       was there
     until it
                 cracked
     and
       I never knew
           what it was
               to fly
               until
                I
                   fell.

isters, and all persons of faith, need to have self-confidence, but they also need to go *beyond* self-confidence to confidence in all the resources God offers for personal and spiritual sustenance. These resources include support from others and trust in God's power to help us. We need to rely on the promise of Isaiah in Isaiah 40:29-31:

> He gives strength to the weary,
> And to him who lacks might He increases power.
> Though youths grow weary and tired,
> And vigorous young men stumble badly,
> Yet those who wait for the LORD
> Will gain new strength;
> They will mount up with wings like eagles,
> They will run and not get tired,
> They will walk and not become weary.

When we rely on this promise, no tragedy can defeat us. We can reach out and risk, having confidence that God will be there for us if we fall. And reaching out and risking is vital to developing a dynamic ministry.

The ultimate reason why divorce often makes a person a better minister is that it forces him or her to let the "Image" fall and to live and minister as a human being. Ministers lose effectiveness when they have to expend energy hiding their "Achilles' heel" in order to live up to that "Image." But perhaps more importantly, people need people to heal their hurts—genuine people with feelings and fallacies. People don't need falsehood covered over with a flawless veneer to give meaning to their very real problems.

Several ministers, in explaining why their ministry has improved since their divorce, referred specifically to the fact that people see them as more real and human. A minister from New York wrote:

> I believe that people realize more the humanity of the pastor. Hence the counseling and preaching are more from the heart experience than the book experience. This is especially true in my case since people have seen a positive change in me. Much of this has to do with the happiness of my second marriage and the more constructive and joyous approach I have toward relationships, beginning with my own.

A minister from New Hampshire shared that part of the reason people have responded positively to him as a divorced minister is that he did not hide his imperfection, his humanity. He wrote:

> I think if I "hid" my sin from them or hid my feelings and that part of my life, they would have less confidence in me. I don't hide divorce

from them. . . . This is part of my story and it also is a story of God's forgiveness and redemption in the life-long process of making me a whole person. With that, they have confidence.

When ministers thus admit their own humanity and sinfulness, they model the truths of grace and forgiveness in a way that our sinful world can understand. We need those truths. We need that honesty.

The "Image" must fall. But it doesn't have to be through the minister divorcing. I would heartily concur with those who have said that, while divorce may make a person a better minister, it is not the best method. There are other ways to let the "Image" fall. And there are many ministers who have taken other paths to affirming their humanity. I saw a good example of this in the movie "Footloose." John Lithgow plays a minister who is trying to be the perfect "father-protector" to all his people. He tries to live the "Image" for some of his parishioners who are trying to control their community by dictating morality. But he is forced to let the "Image" fall because his daughter is human and she needs a human father.

Any event that can get a person to look at his or her own humanity and see more clearly his or her own sinfulness, in all its ugliness, can help that person to be a better minister. This has to go beyond the minister saying, "Yes, I too am a sinner." This may be pseudo-piety and part of the "Image" unless both minister and people can see that the minister's sinfulness is real and not just an abstraction. Unless people see the minister as a sinner (though a forgiven one), that minister may always be too high on a pedestal to be found or to give human touch and healing.

Divorce means many things to the minister. It means death. But it also means resurrection. It means pain. But it can also open up new paths to joy. It means receiving a vital ministry from lay people. But it also means the possibility of giving a revived ministry to them. Most of all, divorce means the "Image" has fallen. For some of us, at least, that much is a relief.

APPENDIX A

Questionnaire for Divorced Ministers

The following summarizes the responses I received to the questionnaire that I distributed to divorced ministers.

Statistical:

Total respondents: 41

1. Sex: male—34; female—7
2. Age: average—46; range—29 to 59
3. Years in ministry: average—21; range—from seminary to 34 years
4. Denominations represented with number of respondents from each denomination:

American Baptist—24 Southern Baptist—2
United Methodist—10 Episcopal—2
Presbyterian—2 U.C.C.—1

5. Relative size of present church versus church at time of divorce:

Now in a larger church—6
Now in a smaller church—12
Now in same size church—4
No response or not applicable—19

6. Years in marriage: average for first marriages—17.7 years; average for second marriages ending in divorce*—3.0 years; overall average—16.5 years.

*There were four cases in which the minister was divorced twice.

7. Time since divorce: average—5.7 years; range—from 0-31 years.

8. Party who filed: minister—24; former spouse—11; cross-filed—4

9. Present marital status: married—25; single—16

Responses to questions (not all respondents answered each item on the questionnaire):

1. Briefly, how does your divorce fit into your present theological perspective?

    Ministers referred to the following concepts in their responses:

    God's forgiveness and grace are available—15
    Divorce is a result of man's failure/sin/imperfection—10
    Divorce falls short of God's intention/ideal—7
    Divorce is sometimes a decision for life, and God is for life—
        3
    God wants us to be fulfilled/to realize our potential—3
    God helps bring good out of bad—3
    Divorce is choosing the lesser of two sins or evils—2
    Divorce is still in conflict with present values and beliefs—2
    Other concepts: Divorce is an opportunity for growth; we are
        not to be legalistic; bad marriages are not God's will; divorce
        is a breach of covenant.

2. How has your divorce affected the quality of your life?

    Of those responding to this item:

    20—said that divorce has improved the quality of their life
     4—indicated that the quality of their life has deteriorated
     6—said that divorce had no effect on the quality or that the
         positive and negative effects balanced out
     8—made no qualitative evaluation

3. How did your divorce affect your self-image?

    Ministers responding to this item made reference to the following changes in their self-image:

    Initially felt like a failure—9
    Had a negative self-image—9
    Had an improved self-image—7

Was helped by others in developing an improved self-image—
5

At first had a worse self-image, but then had a better self-image—
4

Was helped by therapy in developing self-image—4

Had more confidence—3

Felt guilty—3

Saw self differently—3

Self-image was hurt worse by the bad marriage—2

Was relieved at no longer having to live up to the image of
perfection a minister faces—2

Felt unattractive—1

4. Was your church supportive or unsupportive of you at the time of
the divorce? To what extent?

Of those who responded to this item:

26—felt supported by their churches

6—felt that their churches were basically unsupportive

2—felt that the reaction was mixed

In addition, 4 persons in institutional ministry felt basic support,
although one referred to lack of support by the denomination.

5. How specifically have congregations (past and present) shown
support of you as a divorced minister?

Respondents referred to the following actions:

Offering to let them retain a church position—5

Including them socially—4

Not bringing up the divorce or asking personal questions—4

Prayer—3

Acceptance—2

Encouragement—2

Help with children—2

Sharing own experiences—2

Others: checking in on them on holidays; not setting them up
on dates; helping with repairs; encouraging dating.

6. How could the congregation have been more supportive of you and
your marriage *prior* to the divorce?

Of those who responded to this item:

9—thought the church could *not* have been more helpful

6—said that they didn't reveal the problem to the church

3—didn't know what the church could have done

3—said it should have made fewer demands on the family

2—said it should have been more responsive to needs of the family

2—said it could have helped them to get marital counseling

Others: It could have been more supportive of time off; it could have listened more to him and family; it could have been more open to discussing the minister's problems; it could have shown more friendship; it could have been more confrontal about things the minister was doing wrong.

7. Prior to your divorce, did you get marriage counseling? If so, for how long? What effect did it have, if any?

Of those who responded to this item:

25—said they had had marriage counseling

13—said they had not had marriage counseling

Length of counseling varied from a few sessions to over 4 years. The typical response was that counseling helped the minister personally but was not enough to save the marriage.

8. Did your divorce affect your retaining your church position or getting a new one?

Yes—15

No—20

Uncertain—2

9. From your perspective, how has your divorce affected the confidence your parishoners have in you as a counselor and preacher?

Respondents referred to the following attitudes:

Increased confidence because of learnings and experience—14

No effect on confidence—10

Helped in gaining confidence of other divorced people—3

A minority found it hard to accept their ministry—3

Mixed reaction—2

Found self being apologetic—1

Weakened position in these areas—1

10. In your marital counseling, do you (number of respondents are in parentheses):

    a. Advise couples divorce is *always* inappropriate? (0)
    b. Advise couples divorce is appropriate only after every effort has been made to reconcile, including marriage counseling? (26)
    c. Advise couples that if they are unhappy, they should get divorced? (0)
    d. Avoid counseling people one way or another on whether or not they should get divorced? (7)
    e. Other (5)—Responses included encouraging persons to make their own decisions, helping persons solve differences by loving Christ and each other, sharing the minister's own experience and pain.

11. How in general has your divorce affected your ministry?

    Of those responding to this item:

    18—thought that they are better ministers now
    13—thought that they are now more sensitive/nonjudgmental
    6—felt that it helped with ministry with singles
    3—thought that it opened new ministries
    3—believed that it led to lost ministerial opportunities
    3—felt that they make better marriage counselors now
    1—thought that ministry has lost its energy

12. What bearing, if any, did the fact that you are a minister have on the marital problems that led to your divorce?

    The following issues were mentioned:

    Kept me from facing need for divorce—6
    Led to subordinating family to the ministry—6
    Spouse didn't like time spent at church work—6
    Had little or no impact—5
    Spouse was antichurch—4
    Felt pressure to be perfect and live up to the Image—3
    Lack of friends—2
    Spouse didn't like role as minister's wife/husband—2
    Other: Spouse was possessive; church conflicts and family conflicts aggravated each other; parsonage issues; competition between ministers married to each other.

Questionnaire for Ex-Spouses of Ministers

The following summarizes the responses I received to the questionnaire that I distributed to former spouses of ministers.

Statistical:

Total respondents: 7

1. Sex: male—0; Female—7
2. Age: average—52.0; range—39 to 66
3. Years in marriage to a minister: average—25.5; range—16 to 42
4. Time since divorce: average—6.0 years; range—1.5 to 13 years
5. Party who filed: self—3; former spouse—4
6. Present martial status: married—3; single—4
7. State of present residence: Washington—3; Idaho—1; Kentucky—1; Illinois—1; New Mexico—1

Responses to questions:

1. How has your divorce affected the quality of your life?

   Respondents referred to the following effects:

   Gave more freedom—2
   Brought negative self-image—2
   Stimulated thoughts of suicide—1
   Caused poor quality of life—2
   Brought financial/job problems—2
   Brought professional/financial improvement—1

Gave independence—1
Brought opportunity to develop new skills—1
Gave sense of failure—1

2. What issues, if any, do you feel you had to face because you were divorced from a minister, as opposed to a person of another profession?

Respondents referred to the following issues:

Stigma greater when divorced from minister—3
Greater amount of guilt—3
Lack of denominational support—1
Loss of financial benefits—1
Loss of identity—1

3. Was the church supportive or unsupportive of you at the time of the divorce? To what extent?

Supportive—3
Unsupportive—4

4. How could the congregation have been more supportive of you and your marriage *prior* to the divorce?

Needs to which respondents referred included:

Not put me on pedestal and not require me to be perfect—2
More time off for spouse (minister)—1
Less critical of spouse (minister)—1
Affirm me as person—1
Include ministerial family more in the joys of life—1

5. How has your divorce affected your relationship to the church?

Five out of the seven had the experience affect their relationship in a negative way. More specific responses were:

Left church as an institution—3
Have greater awareness of family orientation of church—3
Left denomination—1
Left local church attended previously—6
Distrust church now—1
Married another minister—1
Feel commitment/involvement is not diminished—2

6. What bearing, if any, did the fact that you were married to a minister have on marital problems that led to your divorce?

Respondents referred to the following factors:

Falseness of roles and expectations—2
Former minister-husband placed church before family—3
Lack of outside interests—1
No affect—1

For Further Reading

Bouma, Mary LaGrand, *Divorce in the Parsonage*. Minneapolis: Bethany House Publishers, 1979.

Bridges, William, *Transitions: Making Sense of Life's Changes*. Reading, Mass.: Addison-Wesley Publishing Co., Inc., 1980.

Dahl, Gerald L., *Why Christian Marriages Are Breaking Up*. Nashville: Thomas Nelson, Inc., 1981.

Demarest, Gary, *Christian Alternatives Within Marriage*. Waco, Tex.: Word, Inc., 1977.

Goodling, Richard A., and Smith, Cheryl, "Clergy Divorce: A Survey of Issues and Emerging Ecclesiastical Structures." *The Journal of Pastoral Care*, Vol. 37, December 1983.

Landgraf, John R., *Creative Singlehood and Pastoral Care*. Philadelphia: Fortress Press, 1982.

Mace, David and Vera, *What's Happening to Clergy Marriages?* Nashville: Abingdon Press, 1980.

Malcomson, William L., ed., *How to Survive in the Ministry*. Valley Forge: Judson Press, 1982.

Richards, Larry, *Remarriage*. Waco, Tex.: Word, Inc., 1981.

Sinclair, Donna, *The Pastor's Wife Today*. Nashville: Abingdon Press, 1981.

Stout, Robert J., "Clergy Divorce Spills into the Aisle," *Christianity Today*, Vol. 26 (February 5, 1982).

Warlick, Harold C., Jr., *How to Be a Minister and a Human Being*. Valley Forge: Judson Press, 1982.

Notes

Chapter 1

[1] Kenneth L. Woodward, "Pick-and-Choose Christianity," *Newsweek*, September 19, 1983.

[2] Paul B. Horton and Chester L. Hunt, *Sociology*, 2nd ed. (New York: McGraw-Hill, Inc., 1968), p.225.

[3] Quoted in Donna Sinclair, *The Pastor's Wife Today* (Nashville: Abingdon Press, 1981), p. 80; and Mary LaGrand Bouma, *Divorce in the Parsonage* (Minneapolis: Bethany House Publishers, 1979), p.12.

[4] Richard A. Goodling, and Cheryl Smith, "Clergy Divorce: A Survey of Issues and Emerging Ecclesiastical Structures," *The Journal of Pastoral Care*, vol. 37, December 1983, p.277.

[5] David and Vera Mace, *What's Happening to Clergy Marriages?* (Nashville: Abingdon Press, 1980), p.133.

[6] Bouma, p.44.

[7] Goodling and Smith, p.280.

[8] Robert J. Stout, "Clergy Divorce Spills into the Aisle," *Christianity Today*, vol. 26, February 5, 1982, p.20.

[9] *Ibid*.

[10] *Ibid*.

[11] Mace and Mace, p.55.

[12] See, for example, Goodling and Smith, p.288.

Chapter 2

[1] Raymond Calkins, *The Romance of the Ministry* (New York: The Pilgrim Press, 1944), p.33.

[2] *Ibid.*, pp.35-36.

[3] *Ibid.*, p.38.

[4] David and Vera Mace, *What's Happening to Clergy Marriages?* (Nashville: Abingdon Press, 1980), p.59.

[5] John R. Landgraf, "Fit or Misfit: The Minister's Spouse," in *How to Survive in the Ministry*, ed. William L. Malcomson, (Valley Forge: Judson Press, 1982), p.56.

[6] Mace and Mace, p.58.

[7] Robert J. Stout, "Clergy Divorce Spills into the Aisle," *Christianity Today,* vol. 26, February 5, 1982, p.23.

Chapter 3

[1] Ronald J. Sider and Richard K. Taylor, *Nuclear Holocaust and Christian Hope* (Downers Grove, Ill.: Inter-Varsity Press, 1982), pp.183-184. © 1982 by Ronald J. Sider and Richard K. Taylor and used by permission of Inter-Varsity Press, Downers Grove, IL 60515.

[2] Quoted in David and Vera Mace, *What's Happening to Clergy Marriages?* (Nashville: Abingdon Press, 1980), p.133.

[3] Quoted in Richard A. Goodling, and Cheryl Smith, "Clergy Divorce: A Survey of Issues and Emerging Ecclesiastical Structures," *The Journal of Pastoral Care,* vol. 37, December 1983, p.280.

[4] David J. Juroe and Bonnie B. Juroe, *Successful Stepparenting* (Old Tappan, N.J.: Fleming H. Revell Co., 1983), p.9.

Chapter 4

[1] David and Vera Mace, *What's Happening to Clergy Marriages?* (Nashville: Abingdon Press, 1980), p.59.

[2] *Ibid.*, p.27.

[3] John Landgraf, "Creating Wholeness for the Minister of Tomorrow," in *How to Survive in the Ministry*, ed. William L. Malcomson, (Valley Forge: Judson Press, 1982), p.13.

[4] Donna Sinclair, *The Pastor's Wife Today* (Nashville: Abingdon Press, 1981), p.81.

[5] Marshall Shelley and Dean Merrill, "The Pastor's Passages," *Leadership*, Fall 1983, p.17.

[6] Sinclair, pp.81-85.

[7] Mary LaGrand Bouma, *Divorce in the Parsonage* (Minneapolis: Bethany House Publishers, 1979), p.141.

[8] Quoted in Harold C. Warlick, Jr., *How to Be a Minister and a Human Being* (Valley Forge: Judson Press, 1982), p.105.

[9] Robert J. Stout, "Clergy Divorce Spills into the Aisle," *Christianity Today*, vol. 26, February 5, 1982, p.23.

[10] Quoted in Warlick, pp.34-35.

[11] Michael LeBoeuf, *Imagineering: How to Profit from Your Creative Powers* (New York: McGraw-Hill, Inc., 1980), pp.202-203.

[12] Bouma, p.23.

[13] Stout, p.23.

[14] Mace and Mace, p.130.

[15] Stout, pp.22-23.

[16] "The War Within: An Anatomy of Lust," *Leadership*, Fall 1982, pp.30-48.

[17] Bouma, pp.41-42.

[18] Warlick, p.38.

[19] Janet F. Fishburn, "Male Clergy Adultery as Vocational Confusion," *The Christian Century*, September 15-22, 1982, pp.922-925.

[20] Bouma, p.41.

[21] Stout, p.21.

[22] Mace and Mace, p.39.

Chapter 5

[1] Howard C. Kee, *et al.*, *Understanding the New Testament*, 2nd ed. (Englewood Cliffs, N.J.: Prentice-Hall, Inc., 1965), p.282.
[2] George A. Buttrick, "The Gospel According to St. Matthew," *The Interpreter's Bible*, vol.7 (Nashville: Abingdon Press, 1951), p.291.
[3] Larry Richards, *Remarriage* (Waco, Tex.: Word, Inc., 1981), p.22.
[4] Gary Demarest, *Christian Alternatives Within Marriage* (Waco, Tex.: Word, Inc., 1977), p.47. Used by permission of WORD BOOKS, PUBLISHER, Waco, Texas 76796.

Chapter 6

[1] Elisabeth Kübler-Ross, *On Death and Dying* (New York: Macmillan, Inc., 1970).
[2] William Bridges, *Transitions: Making Sense of Life's Changes* (Reading, Mass.: Addison-Wesley Publishing Co., Inc., 1980).
[3] Gary Demarest, *Christian Alternatives Within Marriage* (Waco, Tex.: Word, Inc., 1977), p.57.

Chapter 7

[1] All of the former spouses who responded to my questionnaire were women. And the studies that I have seen also have dealt exclusively with former wives. In some ways the experiences of former husbands and former wives can be expected to be similar. One report has it that female ministers find the impact of ministry on their spouses to be as difficult as on spouses of male ministers. (See Harold C. Warlick, Jr., *How to be a Minister and a Human Being* [Valley Forge: Judson Press, 1982], p.39.) But in some areas, whether the impact of a divorce on a former husband would be the same as on a former wife is less than obvious. While we are concerned with both former husbands and former wives, the primary reference of our data is former wives.
[2] Richard A. Goodling and Cheryl Smith, "Clergy Divorce: A Survey of Issues and Emerging Ecclesiastical Structures," *The Journal of Pastoral Care*, vol. 37, December 1983, p.285.
[3] Patricia Evans Coots, quoted in *ibid*.
[4] Mary LaGrand Bouma, *Divorce in the Parsonage* (Minneapolis: Bethany House Publishers, 1979), p.95.
[5] Patricia Evans Coots, quoted in Goodling and Smith, p.285.
[6] *Ibid*.
[7] *Ibid*.
[8] Bouma, pp.84-99.

Chapter 8

[1] Quoted in Gerald L. Dahl, *Why Christian Marriages Are Breaking Up* (Nashville: Thomas Nelson, Inc., 1979), p.23.
[2] John R. Landgraf, *Creative Singlehood and Pastoral Care* (Philadelphia: Fortress Press, 1982), p.13.
[3] *Ibid.*, p.xiii.
[4] William Bridges, *Transitions: Making Sense of Life's Changes* (Reading, Mass.: Addison-Wesley, Publishing Co., Inc., 1980).

Chapter 9

[1] Quoted in Richard A. Goodling and Cheryl Smith, "Clergy Divorce: A Survey of Issues and Emerging Ecclesiastical Structures," *The Journal of Pastoral Care*, vol.37, December 1983, p.288.

[2] *Ibid.*

[3] Mary LaGrand Bouma, *Divorce in the Parsonage* (Minneapolis: Bethany House Publishers, 1979), p.43.